DEVELOPING
College Skills
in Students with
Autism
and
ASPERGER'S
SYNDROME

Sarita Freedman
Foreword by Tony Attwood

Jessica Kingsley Publishers
London and Philadelphia

First published in 2010
by Jessica Kingsley Publishers
116 Pentonville Road
London N1 9JB, UK
and
400 Market Street, Suite 400
Philadelphia, PA 19106, USA

www.jkp.com

Copyright © Sarita Freedman 2010
Foreword copyright © Tony Attwood 2010

Library of Congress Cataloging in Publication Data
A CIP catalog record for this book is available from the Library of Congress

British Library Cataloguing in Publication Data
A CIP catalogue record for this book is available from the British Library

ISBN 978 1 84310 917 4

Printed and bound in the United States by
Thomson-Shore, Inc.

Developing College Skills in Students with
Autism and Asperger's Syndrome

of related interest

The Complete Guide To Asperger's Syndrome
Tony Attwood
ISBN 978 1 84310 495 7 (hardback)
ISBN 978 1 84310 669 2 (paperback)

Realizing the College Dream with Autism or Asperger Syndrome
A Parent's Guide to Student Success
Ann Palmer
ISBN 978 1 84310 801 6

Adults on the Autism Spectrum Leave the Nest
Achieving Supported Independence
Nancy Perry
ISBN 978 1 84310 904 4

CONTENTS

PART III: GOING TO COLLEGE

ACKNOWLEDGEMENTS

I would never have been able to write this book without the valuable lessons I learned from the children and adults I've worked with throughout my career. They have taught me the most about autism, and for that I am forever grateful. They are interesting, unique individuals whose perspectives on the world have certainly opened my own mind, as well as the minds of their families. Parents and families of individuals with ASD have great strength and unbelievable stamina in the face of countless roadblocks. They are charged with having to be their child's advocate, all along not truly knowing what the future holds in store for their child because professionals can assure them of nothing. That they and their families allowed me to be a small part of their lives, has been an honor and a blessing. Many thanks to those of you who have encouraged me to forge ahead on this project, and to those who so kindly allowed me to include some of your experiences in this book. If it contributes in any way to even one student's success, then I have accomplished my goal in writing it.

The never-ending love and support of my husband, David, and my daughter, Danielle, means the world to me and made it possible for me to complete this book. I will never forget their understanding and willingness to tolerate my absence on weekends or whenever I had any free time, and to "pick up the slack" of managing our family. While I am saddened by missing out on spending time with you, I know that you are the backbone of my success. There is no way to express my gratitude other than to tell you that I am eternally grateful and blessed to have your love.

Finally, I could not do the work I do without the support of my friends and colleagues. Your ongoing confidence in me dispels any doubts and fears I might have, and has been the force that drives my perseverance on this project. Every single one of you plays an important and unique role in my daily personal and professional life—whether we laugh, commiserate, share experiences, or simply exchange a quick hello in the ever shifting canvases of our lives, it fortifies and sustains me. Your friendship is a gift and your support is essential… Thank you.

I'd like to thank a few people for their particular roles in the culmination of this project. Nathalie Gossett's research efforts were instrumental in identifying the most current thinking on the subject. Her unbelievable organizational skills and spreadsheets saved me countless hours and will continue to aid me in moving my work forward. Years ago Linda Andron-Ostrow invited me to work with her. By generously including me in many autism-related activities and introducing me to key people in the field, she was instrumental in helping me advance my career. I was introduced by Linda to Tony Attwood and have learned a great deal from him over the years. His friendship and support have been invaluable, and it is an honor to have had his input on this project.

FOREWORD

Many adolescents who have autistic spectrum disorders (ASD) have a desire for knowledge, academic achievement and a chance to prove their intellectual ability. They can be both determined and motivated to attend and graduate successfully from college. However, because of the nature of ASD, there will need to be considerable preparation and support in developing college skills. I use the metaphor of embarking on a long journey to a distant destination. Sarita Freedman's book will provide not only a map for the journey, but also a traveller's guide explaining the new culture of college life, who can be an interpreter, what preparations and equipment are needed, the currency exchange of new friendships, travel tips on avoiding exhaustion, how it feels to be overwhelmed or lost, and ways to enjoy the new experiences and sense of achievement.

Going through college is not easy for most students, but those with ASD will have greater difficulties adapting to new routines and expectations, the requirements to become more financially and emotionally independent, and with the organizational aspects of completing assignments. College is also a new social environment and the student with ASD will be expected to work in a student team for some assignments, make new friends and develop a greater sense of self-identity and direction in life.

Sarita Freedman knows all the issues from her extensive clinical experience, being familiar with the academic and theoretical literature, and reading the autobiographies of adults who have ASD. Being a clinician, she also knows how to communicate her knowledge and strategies in a style that will be appreciated by fellow psychologists, parents, high school teachers, college staff and people with ASD. As I read her manuscript, I was frequently smiling, thinking, "Yes, a perfect explanation and sound practical advice." This book identifies the skills that are needed for a successful college career, with strategies that can be implemented many years before enrolment, and advice on the support and understanding needed during the college years.

If you are concerned about a student who has ASD who will be going to, or is enrolled in, college, I strongly recommend that you read this book from cover to cover. There are aspects that you probably never realized would be so important. Forewarned is forearmed, and students with ASD can have a greater degree of confidence preparing for and coping with college life because of the wisdom that both you and they will acquire from Sarita's new book.

Tony Attwood
Minds and Hearts Clinic
Brisbane, Australia

PREFACE

In the early 1990s it began to be understood that the diagnostic category of "autistic disorder" was actually broader than we had originally known. It was, in fact, more of a "spectrum" that included individuals with a broad range of functioning abilities, from severely mentally retarded to highly gifted. Individuals with "autistic spectrum disorder" (ASD) who had cognitive abilities in the average to above average range came to be referred to as "high functioning." Those with Asperger's syndrome (AS) were also considered to be "high functioning" (HF) individuals on the spectrum of autistic disorders. These individuals represented a group of people who were often referred to as "loners" or "eccentric," "exceedingly shy," "awkward," etc. They also represented a group of individuals who, in retrospect, were some of the greatest creators and geniuses of all time. According to the Autism Society of America, individuals with ASD, regardless of their "level of functioning," experience multiple challenges to varying degrees, in verbal and nonverbal communication, leisure or play activities, and social communication.

My first experience of working with children who today would be classified as "high functioning" was as a special education teacher over the course of ten years, beginning in the mid-1970s. I was fortunate enough to have worked in a federally funded preschool education project that was designed to research various intervention techniques and what was then called *reverse mainstreaming*—a school for special needs children where typically developing children from the community are included as a way to build tolerance for differences and to have appropriate language and play role models. The group of children that I worked with were identified as speech and language impaired, but they also exhibited other characteristics that did not fit neatly into any of the available diagnostic criteria at that time, and, as such, were regarded as an enigma. They did, in fact, have delayed language skills, and one of the main areas of deficit was in pragmatic communication (see Chapter 1, p.21). Whether they had some language or were nonverbal, what was noticeable about many in this particular group of children, was that they did not attempt to communicate by any other means (e.g. gesture, eye contact, etc.). They were not curious about the environment, which made it very difficult to engage them in play. However, they did not fall into what at that time was known as "autistic" because they were bright and actually progressed well in most academic areas. I believe these children would have been diagnosed today with autism and would have been considered HF.

As a psychologist beginning my practice in the early 1990s, I had many opportunities to diagnose and treat young children with HF autism, and continued to do so ever since. Several years ago I started getting calls from parents of students who'd already had a rough start in their post-secondary education (PSE) and, as a result, were unsure if they wanted to continue with it or try again.

The idea for this book arose out of an awareness that while current research on the various factors affecting older teens and young adults is currently only in its beginning stages, they need help now. There is a paucity of services available to this older group of HF individuals, primarily because most of the existing service delivery systems were designed to meet the needs of lower functioning individuals. HF students are frequently underserved or fall between the cracks in these systems as a result of under-diagnosis, lack of trained professionals, and/ or funding deficits. In spite of early and ongoing intervention, many students with ASD fall short in areas that are essential to becoming independent young adults and, as such, need ongoing support in order to be successful in life.

This book identifies the distinct and unique needs that most students with ASD entering PSE will have, as well as the many skill sets they need to develop in order to be successful in college and in life. In response to cases that arose within my own clinical practice, these skill sets, and fuller understanding of the most salient issues that could potentially affect a student's success in PSE, were culled from the current research and literature. I also present effective intervention strategies that can be implemented throughout the student's development, and ideally *before* the student begins college.

The primary focus of this book is geared towards a wide variety of professionals who work with students with ASD, including mental health practitioners, high-school administrators, high-school career counselors, college placement specialists, educational therapists, speech and language pathologists, individuals at state Disabilities Services Offices, vocational rehabilitation counselors, and Disabilities Services Advisors at PSE institutions. However, it will also be useful to parents and other primary caregivers who interface with these professionals and can influence the direction of the student's intervention program. Older individuals with ASD who want to build on, or extend their independent living skills, may also be interested in this book. Please note that in writing the book, I assume that the reader is already familiar with ASD, and so diagnostic and characteristic concepts will not be addressed in great detail. There are a plethora of excellent books available for those who want introductory material.

In addressing the needs of students with ASD who have the capability to embark on PSE, the recommendations in this book focus on the HF group of individuals diagnosed with ASD. However, every student is unique, whether they are typically developing or not. Therefore, the ideas and suggestions in this book are not meant to be prescriptive for *all* students. The types of accommodations (i.e. modifications to the learning environment and/or coursework) and interventions (see Chapter 10) that any particular student may require to be successful in college and beyond should address that student's individual profile of abilities and areas of need. By identifying key areas of need, professionals will be better equipped to help develop the types of skills that individual students will need in order to have a positive PSE experience.

Many post-secondary programs are already answering the call to provide innovative, structured and not-so-structured programs so that students with ASD can realize their full potential and become valuable contributors to our society. But clearly more research has to be done to enable students with ASD to succeed both in their PSE and throughout their lifespan. I hope that this text serves both to reinforce the valuable information that is already available, and to extend the existing knowledge base about this topic. I also hope that the tools provided in the text will ultimately serve its purpose—to prepare individuals with ASD to succeed in college and beyond.

The chapters in this book are organized in the following manner. In Part I, Chapter 1 aims to help the reader understand the many facets of autism spectrum disorders across the lifespan. A discussion about the term *high functioning*, as it applies to ASD, is also included. In Part II, Chapters 2–8 focus on individual skill sets that will enable students to achieve success in PSE and beyond. Some of these skill sets were identified in the research and self-help literature, and others were included from the author's professional experience. Skill sets are described in detail, and included in the discussion are various ideas for developing them, often beginning when children are as young as three years of age, and certainly prior to leaving home for college. In Part III, Chapters 9–11 highlight numerous factors to consider about pursuing a college education, including an overview of the laws pertaining to equal access for individuals with disabilities. Also presented are classroom and teaching strategies, and ideas for making necessary, system-wide changes so that future students can be better prepared for their adult lives. Finally, there are two appendices, including a table of skill sets and a list of helpful resources and websites.

PART I
The Many Facets of Autism

Chapter 1

BECOMING FAMILIAR WITH AUTISM

WHAT IS AUTISM?

Autism is a neurodevelopmental disorder that manifests as impairments in three primary areas of functioning: communication and play, social relatedness, and restricted interests and activities. The *Diagnostic and Statistical Manual of Mental Disorders*, Fourth Edition (DSM-IV) (American Psychiatric Association 1994a) details the diagnostic criteria for all of the pervasive developmental disorders, including autistic disorder, Rett's disorder, childhood disintegrative disorder, Asperger's syndrome, and pervasive developmental disorder, not otherwise specified. The reader is referred to the most recent edition of the DSM for full diagnostic criteria. This book examines the needs of individuals in three of the primary diagnostic categories: autistic disorder, Asperger's syndrome, and pervasive developmental disorder, not otherwise specified (PDD-NOS). The general diagnostic criteria for autistic disorder are given below.

Impairments in social relatedness including deficits in any of four primary areas:

- nonverbal communication (e.g. eye contact, reading nonverbal cues)
- peer interaction (does not develop developmentally appropriate peer relationships)
- joint attention (does not seek to share enjoyment; no showing or pointing out of objects of interest)
- emotional reciprocity (does not exhibit shared emotional experiences with others).

Impairments in communication in play including deficits in any of four primary areas:

- delays in, or lack of language development (without compensating with gestures or sounds)
- impaired ability to sustain conversation
- stereotyped or repetitive language use (includes idiosyncratic language)
- lack of varied spontaneous make-believe play or social imitative play.

Restricted and repetitive or stereotyped play, interests, or activities:

- preoccupations and interests that are abnormal in intensity and/or focus
- inflexible adherence to specific, nonfunctional routines and/or rituals
- motor stereotypes (e.g. hand/finger flapping or flicking, repetitive jumping, complex body movements)
- preoccupation with parts of objects (e.g. only spins wheels on cars; takes clocks apart to study the mechanism but has no interest in telling time; visually scrutinizes and examines objects without concomitant appropriate play with the object).

The diagnostic criteria for Asperger's syndrome are identical except in the area of communication, where it is expected that there are no significant delays in overall language development, cognitive development, "or in the development of age appropriate self-help skills, adaptive behavior (other than in social interaction) and curiosity about the environment in childhood" (American Psychiatric Association 1994b, p.62). For both disorders it is expected that the delays and impairments in at least one of the listed areas had their onset prior to the age of three. Individuals in the PDD-NOS category can exhibit difficulties with reciprocal social interactions, verbal or nonverbal communication, and/or stereotyped behavior, interests and activities. This category includes individuals who do not meet the required criteria for a diagnosis of autistic or Asperger's syndrome, those in whom the onset was later than age three, and those whose symptoms are atypical or subclinical (American Psychiatric Association 1994b, p.62).

In the body of this text, the term autism spectrum disorder (ASD) is used to refer to individuals who fall under the broad diagnostic umbrella of the pervasive developmental disorders (autistic disorder, Asperger's disorder, and PDD-NOS).

WHAT DOES ASD LOOK LIKE?

The most obvious initial observations are that *social initiations are less play-based and more directed towards adults.* Most of the child's interactions are based on getting personal needs met, rather than to engage another person. We see *reduced or no joint attention and social referencing,* and a reduction in the individual's awareness and/or response to others' emotional distress. Joint attention relates to two (or more) individuals attending to the same object and recognizing a shared experience. Social referencing relates to learning by watching the expression on someone's face or listening to another person's tone of voice. For example, when a baby reaches for a novel object, the baby may look towards the mother and, by "reading" the expression on her face, determine whether or not it is safe to take or touch the object. Similarly, another person's tone of voice can affect the decision a child makes in many situations, but the child with ASD may be unable to discern subtle changes in tone of voice. Individuals with ASD have a significantly reduced ability to read nonverbal cues, including facial expressions and gestures, and they also tend to exhibit fewer nonverbal cues and gestures than would normally be expected.

As a result of the above-mentioned challenges, students with ASD must learn how to interact successfully with others in an intellectual and cognitive manner. With the appropriate level and intensity of intervention throughout their development, most HF individuals will be able to learn these skills. In the absence of social skills the incredibly sophisticated and complex social world will remain a mystery, and the student will flounder when engaging in activities with others. Imagine the challenge of dorm living, or working as part of a group project, with limited ability to be aware of and respond to others, or without the ability to read facial expressions and other nonverbal cues.

Motor functioning is usually impaired to varying degrees, and graphomotor (writing) skills are almost always impaired. With the advent of technology and computers in both of which many individuals with ASD are highly competent, graphomotor challenges will likely present a rather minor disturbance or annoyance. There is also an almost universally *abnormal response to sensory stimuli* such as sound, touch, and light—factors that can pose significant obstacles in the ever changing and fluid environment of a college campus. In their study on sensory processing deficits in adults with ASD, Crane, Goddard and Pring (2009) found that 94.4 percent of the sampled adults with ASD reported varying types of sensory processing abnormalities, albeit at "similarly severe" levels. Their results "suggest that unusual sensory processing in ASD extends across the lifespan" (p.215). Impairments in sensory processing can also result in unusually modulated behavior and tone of voice (e.g. flattened or overly loud). Finally, individuals with ASD *struggle to attach emotion to environmental stimuli*, hence the *lack of awareness of danger* (e.g. touching a hot stove and getting burned doesn't necessarily mean the behavior won't happen again). They also attach emotion to stimuli that to typically developing people may appear benign (e.g. intense fears of normally benign objects or events). Both of these restrictions pose challenges in the area of learning while doing, and generalization of learning from one situation to another.

One of the most significant areas of impairment falls in what is known as *executive functioning* (EF), a set of brain-based activities that include:

- cognitive flexibility
- inhibition of irrelevant responses

- behavioral adaptation to environment
- understanding codes of conduct
- using experience to understand rules
- identifying essential from nonessential information
- ability to retain a goal and the steps needed to accomplish it in one's mind (working memory).

These challenges can significantly impair individual ability to initiate and complete numerous tasks (e.g. decide which toy to play with; select a topic for a school project; organize activities such as book reports and long-term projects). As a result, they can get stuck in counterproductive routines and have trouble in learning from their experiences. Individuals who are severely challenged in the area of EF struggle a great deal with college activities. However, individuals with ASD do quite well with routine and structure, and they can also learn compensatory strategies such as using activity charts, a calendar, or a whiteboard to map out the steps needed to complete a project. These strengths will enable them to master many of their challenges.

Social communication and language difficulties may manifest as talking about topics of specific interest, difficulty in changing the topic of conversation, difficulty in reading the listener's cues for interest (or lack of it) in the conversation, and/or limited ability for conversational turn-taking. Some individuals with ASD will also exhibit differences in voice pitch and inflection, also referred to as "prosody." Because they tend to be concrete thinkers, people with ASD often take things they hear literally, and have trouble understanding humor and sarcasm.

Another area of significant language impairment lies in *pragmatic communication*, a component of speech and language development that is usually treated by speech and language pathologists. While this is an extremely important skill for all students, it falls into the area of speech and language pathology and will not be included in the skills chapters. However, I cannot overemphasize the importance of ensuring that students are relatively proficient in pragmatic communication. Here are the skills that need to be focused on (Legrand 2001, personal communication):

- Knowing that you have to answer when a question has been asked. This skill involves also knowing how to ask for clarification if you don't understand a question, are confused, or there's a communication breakdown.

- Being able to participate in a conversation by taking turns with the other speaker. This involves recognizing when the other speaker has finished talking and, if unsure, asking the speaker if he or she has finished. It also requires the individual to appreciate and understand the purpose of sharing information (related to joint attention).

- Noticing and responding appropriately to the nonverbal aspects of language.

- Knowing that you have to introduce a topic of conversation in order for the listener to understand fully what you will be talking about, and that you have to check for understanding throughout your conversations.

- Knowing which words or what sort of sentence-type to use when initiating a conversation or responding to something someone has said.

- Knowing how to end a conversation appropriately.

- Knowing how to ask for clarification when you don't understand something.

- Knowing how to provide clarification so that the listener understands you: this includes being able to "read" the listener's facial expression to know if the listener is following you.

- Knowing the importance of staying on topic, and being able to do so.

- Maintaining appropriate eye contact (not too much staring, and not too much looking away) during a conversation.

- Being able to distinguish how to talk and behave towards different communication partners.

Most of the people I work with have needed intervention in this area. A referral to a speech and language pathologist who has been trained in the area of pragmatics is appropriate when working with individuals with ASD, no matter what their age. Pragmatic skills become more and more sophisticated throughout life and it is useful for high-school students and young adults to work with a speech and language pathologist in order to keep up with the communication rules and strategies of their peer groups.

Inability to read nonverbal cues is one of the most challenging areas for students with ASD, and ties into the skills needed for pragmatic communication. Not only is it important for students to understand body language for conversation, body language also provides us with a great deal of very valuable information regarding mental states (e.g. intentions, perspectives, beliefs) and, most important, deception. Most individuals with ASD are baffled by deception and have a hard time accepting that others would want to fool, trick, or harm them. According to Chitale (2008), the "guileless and trusting" stance of individuals with ASD makes them "prime targets for abuse, thievery and scams. According to the Department of Justice, people with developmental disabilities, including autism, have a four to ten times higher risk of becoming crime victims and are twice as likely to be sexually abused as people without those disabilities" (p.1).

Because of their poor communication skills, individuals with ASD may be unable to disclose abuse. They are easily influenced and may be reluctant to disclose abuse for fear of something terrible happening to them or a family member. Tragically, children with ASD who have been sexually abused but do not have the psychological maturity to work through issues of abuse often develop hyper-sexualized behavior and can ultimately be accused, themselves, of perpetrating sexual abuse. All of the women with ASD that I've worked with have had some sort of inappropriate sexual experience, from being touched inappropriately as a child to being the victim of rape as a result of not being able to "read" the perpetrator's intentions. Many women report that they continue to feel unsafe and uncomfortable because their ability to detect this type of deception is seriously underdeveloped. Males also share this deficit and are also at risk for sexual exploitation. HF individuals will undoubtedly be exposed to issues of sexuality during the course of their lives, including crushes, dating, and marriage. Providing them with specific instruction in these areas may be the only way to keep them safe.

Theory of Mind (ToM) is an area in which most HF individuals with ASD exhibit mild to moderate levels of impairment. ToM is the ability to understand and attribute various mental states, including emotions, beliefs, desires, intentions, and perceptions—both to oneself, and to others. It is a form of "mind-reading" that evolves over time in typical development. We use ToM to understand behavior and intentions (our own and that of others), and to predict the effect our own emotions, beliefs, desires, intentions, and perceptions will have on others. There is an intimate interface between ToM and the ability to understand and read nonverbal cues, body language and facial expressions, and deficits in one or more of these areas usually lead to deficits in all of them. An excellent resource for understanding the developmental underpinnings of ToM is Howlin, Baron-Cohen and Hadwin (1999). These authors also explore how deficits in ToM affect our ability to understand deception, empathy, persuasion, and self-consciousness. Important effects of a deficit in ToM include:

- difficulty understanding the unwritten rules of social interaction
- difficulty understanding the thoughts, feelings, and perceptions of the person with whom one is interacting
- inability to provide enough background information for the listener to follow one's train of thought
- taking idioms and other expressions literally
- inability to understand "white lies"
- difficulty understanding deceit and persuasion, with resulting increasing vulnerability to victimization.

ToM remains a difficult area to develop and master. Suggestions for improvement will be presented in Part II.

Reading comprehension difficulties are often identified in many children with ASD, once reading material advances to multiple plots and relationships, more abstract material, and content that requires making inferences. According to Iland (2008), students can have trouble relating what they've read to information they already know, identifying cause and effect, and interpreting a character's behavior and feelings from the text. Many students find it difficult to predict what happens next, and to highlight important aspects of the material (e.g. when needing to write a book report or essay). Iland recommends that college students purchase used text books that have already been highlighted by another student. However, students need to know that they still have to read the material, because the previous student may have missed something important. Understanding the perspectives of different characters and using that information to get an overall gestalt of relationships in the story can also be very challenging, and linguistic idioms can be extremely difficult for students who think literally. Red flags that suggest a student is struggling with comprehension include: trouble answering questions after reading a text, struggling to understand abstract concepts, inability to write about what was read, trouble following or understanding directions. If, any time after the second grade, a student should exhibit any of these problems, he or she should be referred for assessment by both a reading and a speech and language specialist.

Restricted interests or activities can contribute to a variety of problems in different areas. First and foremost, individuals who have highly restricted interests or activities usually struggle with shared social interest and joint attention. Their knowledge base can be deep in one area but shallow in many others, restricting their general knowledge and reference capacity. This can sometimes appear as "poverty of experience," when in actuality they have a wealth of knowledge, but only in their restricted interest area (Iland 2008). Addressing this in treatment can be challenging, and attempting to eliminate the individual's area of interest is not recommended. In fact, many individuals have been able to exploit their specific areas of interest as career opportunities. However, they do need to understand that if they want to succeed in school and in life, it is important to learn how to compartmentalize, or "store" their thoughts (about the specific interest) away during school, in most conversations, and at other times when they need to learn without interference.

Behaviorally, individuals with ASD have trouble tolerating unexpected events, behaviors, or unanticipated shifts. Transitioning between tasks and/or events is often difficult for them, even if the transition is planned. Often when a desired event is imminent, it becomes difficult to focus and stay in the moment because the desired event distracts the individual's thought processes. Once it's time to stop an enjoyable or preferred activity, stress can occur. Conversely, it can be very difficult to engage an individual in a non-preferred task. Because individuals with ASD are logic-oriented, helping them understand the benefits of either participating in a non-preferred task or moving on from a preferred task can go a long way towards gaining cooperation. Finally, intense emotions can be dysregulating to individuals with ASD, meaning that they can become overwhelmed and overloaded. When this happens, it is usually difficult for them to express themselves appropriately, or they may become aggressive or extremely withdrawn. However, most of the people I work with feel appropriately remorseful after an outburst, especially when they understand the impact that their behavior has had on others around them.

MYTHS ABOUT AUTISM

One of the common myths about autism is that individuals with ASD are unable to be empathic. Empathy is the ability to put yourself in someone else's shoes, and individuals with ASD do have the capacity for empathy. Some individuals with ASD report feeling other people's emotions so strongly that their only option is to retreat from the situation because they lack coping skills for handling these intense emotions. It is possible that emotional coping mechanisms are compromised in some individuals with ASD. This may be related to the inability to regulate oneself in overstimulating situations, resulting in intense anxiety and fear. Retreating from the emotional reactions of others can be misunderstood, and often others perceive this as being cold or insensitive. Because their reactions to situations can be unique, filtered through a limited ability to read nonverbal cues, rigid information processing style, and logical thinking, their behavior is often misinterpreted as lack of empathy.

Non-autistic family members often express concern about the capacity of a relative with ASD for empathy when a death in the family occurs. They struggle to understand their relative's grieving process (or lack thereof) because it can be very short in duration. From the logical perspective of someone with ASD, loss is a natural part of life and as such is expectable, thus diminishing their "need" to feel sad for extended periods of time, but not diminishing their sadness. Another example of what can appear to be a "disturbance" in empathy is as follows: some people with ASD are noted to laugh when others are crying, a reaction seemingly inappropriate to the situation. However, people with ASD often report that laughter occurs involuntarily when they are overcome with intense emotion, such as when someone else is crying. Their emotion is, in fact, empathic but is expressed in a socially atypical manner. Finally, individuals with ASD are very forthright in their perceptions. They "speak the truth" but may not realize that what they say could be hurtful to another person. The fact that people with ASD may not express empathy and emotional understanding in the same way that "neurotypical" individuals do, does not minimize their ability to experience deep, personal emotions and empathy (Freedman 2007).

In a recent study on empathy in adults with AS, Dziobek *et al.* (2008) describe empathy as "a multidimensional construct consisting of cognitive…and emotional…components" (p.464). Cognitive empathy is defined as "the capacity to take the perspective of another person and to interpret their mental states" (p.464). It is very much related to the concept of *Theory of Mind*, which is known to be impacted in ASD. Emotional or affective empathy is "defined as an observer's emotional response to another person's emotional state" (p.464). Dziobek *et al.* note that although individuals with AS exhibited impairments in cognitive empathy, they did not differ from the control group in emotional empathy, nor were there differences between the groups in "level of emotional arousability and socially desirable answer tendencies" (p.464). Whether these findings can be generalized to the entire spectrum of individuals with ASD is yet to be determined, but the findings do shed light on a number of important characteristics of empathy, differences in responsiveness between neurotypical individuals and individuals with AS, and reasons why some individuals with ASD might be perceived as lacking empathy. There is also some debate in the professional community about whether or not both cognitive and emotional empathy are necessary in order for their experience to be deemed truly empathic (Gaus 2007).

Another commonly held belief or myth is that people with ASD are not affectionate and, as such, have an attachment disorder or experience lower levels of attachment. To the contrary, there are numerous reports from family members that they are very affectionate with family members, and numerous reports from adults with ASD about feeling affection towards other important individuals, including "significant others." The question then becomes, does affection need to be physically or outwardly expressed in order for it to exist within a person? In discussing her strong feelings of attachment and loss, Donna Williams (2008) notes her "deep attachment to objects, to places, their sensory experiences and layout, and the strong emotional loss in moving house or losing valued attachment objects" (p.2). She further states, "It's important to remember that attachment and loss aren't just externally expressed realities. They can also be internally sensed ones, even preconscious ones, long before we understand our feelings and even longer before we find emotional safety, want, need or reason to share the expression of that" (p.2).

There is a commonly held perception of people with ASD as appearing aloof, which brings into question whether they are interested in others and whether they can have intimate as well as non-intimate relationships. There is also a debate in the professional community about whether people with classic autism are less interested in others than people with AS. From my clinical experience, I have seen HF individuals with both classic autistic symptoms and AS who yearn for friends, and others who do not. In those who do seek relationships, the complexities of social pragmatic communication and other information-processing deficits often interfere in their ability to interact successfully with others, and also in their capacity to have a complete empathic experience (Gaus 2007). Finally, in spite of the fact that romantic relationships can be problematic for many individuals with ASD, there are many who date, and ultimately marry. While these relationships can be rocky (as can relationships between "neurotypical" people), with appropriate guidance and a great deal of patience, the individual with ASD can learn to respond empathically to their significant other. While at first responsiveness can appear to be rote-like, with practice it can become more genuine.

TRUTHS ABOUT PEOPLE WITH ASD

While I am sure that professionals who work closely with this population are well aware of their many strengths and unique qualities, others who do not come in close contact with them unfortunately do not. One of the things I find most refreshing about the people I know and work with is their sense of humor. Although a common characteristic in young students is that they don't always understand jokes or sarcasm, many young people, and especially adults, develop a sense of humor that is both wry and distinctive, especially when they apply their sometimes literal interpretation of the world to humorous observations. Individuals with ASD who do have a good sense of humor can often use it to their advantage because it endears them to others. Conversely, those who struggle to understand humor and sarcasm often feel confused and find themselves not understanding, or even misunderstanding, their interpersonal experiences.

People with ASD are extremely honest, sometimes to a fault. They are the truth-sayers of our world and, as such, do not play (or know how to play) the kinds of "games" that the rest of us instinctively learn. For example, if they are attracted to someone, they are likely to let that person know in an awkwardly straightforward way, and usually in a manner that feels like it's too soon for normal social convention. This may be off-putting to the other party and result in rejection. Similarly, if they do not like something they do not hesitate to say so, which, again, is usually considered socially inappropriate. We see this frequently when children receive a gift that they don't want or like. Children with ASD often have a longer learning curve (compared to typically developing children) for understanding that they need to accept gifts graciously because the significance of a gift lies in the thought that went into it, not the actual gift itself (which can usually be returned or exchanged). The inability to censor oneself has many implications for interpersonal conflict and confusion, both for the person with ASD and for others interacting with that person.

Most of the older teens and young adults that come to my office are very appreciative and desirous of professional assistance. They have usually attained a level of awareness about their challenges but have no idea how to effect change in themselves. When progress is slow, it's important to remember that the client's consistent attendance is more than likely a sign that he or she is benefiting. People with ASD will resist or refuse to do something that they see no purpose in doing. Once they are committed to anything (e.g. treatment, going to class, working), they are consistent, show up on time, and participate willingly. For this reason they also make excellent employees.

The most important key to a successful working relationship with an individual with ASD is trust. When therapists, mentors, advisors, friends, etc., can develop a good rapport with the individual, he or she usually responds positively to suggestions and interventions. I have on several occasions had clients who return to a session saying they did everything I suggested and reporting in great detail what worked and what didn't. For a clinician, this is a gift! While at times these clients can be somewhat stubborn or resistant to trying things that they think are elementary, they are willing to go through a process of attempting to understand their stubbornness, seeing the role it may play in other aspects of their lives, and working through it to achieve greater cooperation.

One of the things I worry about as a clinician is the tremendous vulnerability of these clients. They can be easily exploited, and care must be taken to ensure that this does not happen. For example, the client can feel so much trust and comfort in the treatment that he may agree to do something for fear of disappointing the therapist and losing the relationship. This could prove disastrous and harmful in the hands of an unscrupulous person, and it is important for all professionals who work with ASD clients to be mindful of it.

Finally, people with ASD have a wonderfully creative way of viewing the world. If one attends closely, one's world view can shift as a result of seeing things through their eyes. They detest social injustices and are stymied by lying and deceit… One has to wonder what kind of world we would live in if we, too, could truly embrace these perspectives.

WHAT DOES "HIGH FUNCTIONING" MEAN?

As mentioned previously, this book deals with the "high functioning" individual with ASD. Although this term currently has no behavioral descriptors attached to it, after the inclusion of AS in the DSM-IV in 1994 it became apparent that approximately one-third (and possibly more) of individuals with AS have an IQ in the average to above average range, and so the term "high functioning" is applied to individuals who present with an overall profile of impairments that are much milder than those typically seen in individuals with "classic" autism and some level of mental retardation. Because there are currently no specific guidelines for diagnosing high functioning autism (Attwood 2007), it is simply a descriptive term that can be applied to individuals in all three categories: autistic disorder, AS, and PDD-NOS.

HIGH FUNCTIONING AUTISM VS. ASPERGER'S SYNDROME

Several researchers have attempted to identify differences in cognitive profiles, adaptive functioning levels, and language development (see Klin, Volkmar and Sparrow 2000). However, according to Attwood (2007), "the number of studies that found a difference in cognitive, social, motor or neuropsychological tasks probably equal those indicating no difference" (p.45). Dr. Attwood also notes that in Europe and Australia these terms are used interchangeably.

Because the differences are as yet not clearly defined and are frequently debated, there are multiple diagnostic issues that lead to misdiagnosis or over-diagnosis of one or the other. One factor that can contribute to this is a lack of formal training. Diagnosing ASD requires not only didactic learning, but also extensive experience with numerous individuals on the autistic spectrum. Training can affect one's ability to truly differentiate between the two disorders (by DSM-IV TR standards; see American Psychiatric Association 2000) and may result in under-diagnosis of, for example, autistic disorder, which may be missed when diagnosing a fully verbal and functioning adult if the parents are either unavailable or don't remember their child's development prior to the age of three. Finally, failing to conduct a complete evaluation can result in misdiagnosis and under-diagnosis. For example, a HF ten-year-old can be misdiagnosed with AS if a complete developmental evaluation is not completed to determine whether the child exhibited language delays during the first three to five years of life.

The bigger question is, why does it matter? Accurate diagnosis is essential and usually drives treatment protocol. Therefore, anyone who is misdiagnosed will not receive the appropriate treatment, and this can be tragic in the case of ASD. Diagnosis also, unfortunately, drives service delivery options. In some areas of the United States, a diagnosis of AS can often preclude the child's chances of receiving government support services. While this decision is primarily based on dollars and cents, it has become a source of concern for clinicians and parents. Clinicians may be in an especially difficult position because the guidelines for differential diagnosis at this point in time can be subject to interpretation and are not highly specific. Parents are also in a difficult position because, while they don't wish for their child to have a diagnosis at all, they may also know which diagnoses will make their child eligible for services. It is to be hoped that ongoing research efforts will lead to improvements in available diagnostic systems and enhanced professional training so that services can be available to all who are in need, rather than only to those who receive the appropriate label.

CAN INDIVIDUALS WITH ASD HAVE OTHER TYPES OF PROBLEMS?

Individuals with ASD are as likely to experience other types of medical conditions as those without ASD. We do find increased rates of co-morbid psychiatric conditions in people with ASD, especially in adolescence and adulthood. Anxiety is the most common co-morbid condition, with depression following closely. Barring future identification of structural differences in the cerebral cortices of people with ASD that would contribute to anxiety or depressive conditions, from a clinical perspective it makes sense that they would feel anxious and depressed. They struggle to understand others around them, they frequently experience failure around others, they often know that they're different from others, they can be victims of teasing and bullying, they have a limited social support system and experience frequent social rejection, and they often feel misunderstood. When seeking assistance for an individual with ASD, it is important, first and foremost, to find a professional with expertise in ASD. There are many stories of failed treatment, be it psychological, psychiatric, educational, or otherwise, due to the fact that the treatment provider was unfamiliar with the intricacies of working with ASD. If you are a professional who has not had any training and are treating someone with ASD, please consult with a colleague who has expertise in the area. You will be helping your client immensely, and the knowledge you gain will help you with future clients.

LIFESPAN CHARACTERISTICS OF "HIGH FUNCTIONING" PEOPLE WITH ASD
The first year of life
So how does ASD manifest over the lifespan of an individual? During the first year of life it can be very difficult to detect many developmental

or behavioral abnormalities, although trained professionals in the field are becoming more and more adept at identifying developmental "red flags" in infants. In fact, early identification has become one of the most highly researched areas, with the assumption that the earlier intervention begins, the better the prognosis, and there are numerous websites that parents and professionals can access to learn about early indicators of ASD (see Appendix B). One of the diagnostic challenges during the first year of life is that a baby may exhibit general developmental delays that are not so behaviorally distinct from those in babies who also have mental retardation, making differential diagnosis at this age difficult. However, there are several early "red flag" warnings for ASD, including:

- failing to respond to one's name
- lack of curiosity about the environment and developmentally appropriate toys
- no babbling, pointing or use of gesture by 12 months
- no single words by 16 months, or no two-word spontaneous phrases by 24 months
- loss of language, motor or social skills at any age
- lack of social smiling
- no imitation
- using another person's body for communication (such as using the parent's or teacher's hand to point at a picture in a book or to pour sand from one container to another)
- lack of declarative pointing to objects of interest and looking to share interest and attention with another person (joint attention).

In children with other developmental delays (e.g. mental retardation, specific language delay) but without autism, we would expect to see the development of shared attention at some point later in the child's development (around two to three years of age). Although this makes diagnosis in the first three years of life difficult, it can alert parents and professionals to the need for intervention, regardless of the diagnosis. Once a child reaches 12 months of age, ASD can be more accurately diagnosed by a clinician who specializes in ASD.

The preschool years

In the preschool years behavior patterns consistent with ASD become obvious, albeit with enormous individual variation. Language learning is delayed or not acquired, and concerns about the child's hearing ability will already have been suspected and/or ruled out. Additionally, the child is not using other means, such as gesture or verbalization, to communicate with meaningful intent. If language is present, it can be highly restricted to topics of interest, and usually lacks true communicative intent (e.g. the child labels many objects but rarely engages in reciprocal communication with parents). Social interactions are severely limited, with an absence of imaginative or pretend play such as would be appropriate for this level of development. Overall, the child may act as if others do not exist. The child may exhibit fixations on apparently meaningless activities or objects, such as spinning things or carrying around unusual objects, and experiences tremendous difficulty when asked to give these up. Intolerance to changes in routine becomes quite evident.

Elementary school

In the elementary school years we often see improvements, especially if the child has had intensive early intervention. Overall level of language and cognitive ability make a great difference in progress and prognosis. Children with AS reportedly speak fluently by age five, although their use of language may be odd and they develop what is known as "pedantic speech," which makes them sound like little professors. Interest in others often develops, although social skills are deficient when compared to same-age, typically developing peers. Many children will become confused by their peers' intentions. For example, a peer may have inadvertently bumped into the child and the child misinterprets this as aggression. Humor and sarcasm can also be confusing and misinterpreted as criticism. These are early indicators of deficits in Theory of Mind.

Some children with autistic disorder may still appear to be lower functioning at this age, primarily because they have not yet developed language. However, I have known and also heard of many nonverbal children who do begin to talk between the ages of eight and eleven, surprising both parents and professionals with the sudden shift from what appeared to be "low" functioning to "high" functioning. In children who remain nonverbal, their level of functioning and ability to communicate become more evident if and when they are able to use alternative means of communication. It is sad that, by mid-elementary school, some parents report that their child is never invited to birthday parties or on play dates.

Adolescence

It is commonly held that in adolescence the differences between high functioning autism and AS begin to get blurred. At this stage individuals begin to realize that they are different, which can often lead to depression. In a recent study examining levels of depression in individuals with ASD, Sterling *et al.* (2008) noted that "…the group of individuals who endorsed symptoms of depression was significantly older than those who did not" (p.1016), and so it appears either that depressive symptoms increase with age, or that the more mature an individual becomes, the more his or her awareness of depression increases. With age come increasingly more sophisticated social expectations that the individual perhaps cannot meet, because they lack the necessary adaptive or EF skills. They feel excluded and say things like, "My brain doesn't work like other people's brains," or "No matter how hard I try, I just can't _____." While depression in this population is understandable, increasing self-awareness and self-acceptance can go a long way towards mitigating depression. One way or another, depressive symptoms warrant immediate treatment so that the student can spend the years before college developing the necessary skills and strengthening his or her sense of self.

Because they have a hard time putting their knowledge and experience together to make meaning, it can seem as if people with ASD possess much unconnected information. Having a limited ability to learn from experience and/or to generalize one's learning from one situation to another makes it difficult to feel safe in, and meet the multiple expectations of, the fluid environment that is a college campus. The individual's knowledge base can also appear to be fragmented as a result of knowing many facts about specific topics, with gaps in knowledge about topics of less interest to the individual. Their way of sharing knowledge can also be off-putting, since it may feel as if the individual is talking "at" others rather than "with" them.

It is at this stage of development that parents, teachers, and other professionals worry about the adolescent's overall lack of common sense and recognize how easy it would be for the individual to be victimized or taken advantage of. It becomes clear that teens with ASD have a very difficult time navigating their increasingly complicated social worlds, often resulting in extended periods of time playing video or hand-held games, perhaps to avoid the discomfort and disappointment of repeated social failures. Speech issues are often more obvious in that differences in rate, rhythm, tone, and volume truly stand out—it's no longer "cute," and uniqueness is less desirable than conforming at this stage of development. While communication deficits can appear slight in individuals with high verbal skills, careful examination proves otherwise. Deficits in pragmatics and conversation skills make it difficult to have a reciprocal exchange. Inappropriate body language, including minimal use of facial and other gestures, awkward eye contact (either fleeting or piercing), and poor boundaries, including standing too close when speaking to others, highlight the individual's challenges. Interpreting language literally and misunderstanding slang, idioms, humor, and sarcasm can lead to potential victimization. All of these characteristics and areas of challenge can make it increasingly uncomfortable for others to interact with individuals with ASD because their communication style is so divergent from standard communication protocol.

Adulthood

During adulthood, many HF individuals with ASD function well and excel in their chosen field of study or career path. While they may not have the same kind of social life as their contemporaries, they may have a couple of good friends and feel satisfied with their lives, overall. Some choose to be in an intimate relationship or to marry, and others choose not to.

There are also individuals who superficially appear well adapted and successful, but, although their routine social interactions appear to be intact, continue to be extremely egocentric and isolated, so that it is difficult for them to enter into and maintain deeper interpersonal relationships. Their idiosyncrasies, egocentric bluntness, and fragility can also make it difficult for them to live and work with others. The manner in which they express themselves can be unusual, and they may appear odd in their dress and demeanor. Females may not fit neatly into feminine stereotypes. As a result, they may be perceived as particularly odd in the workplace. It is often difficult for both males and females to make "small talk," and their use of language and gesture, including facial expression, can be stilted. While communication deficits are common, with the right conditions and interventions many individuals with ASD are nevertheless able to achieve success and satisfaction.

Deficits in Theory of Mind probably have the most negative impact as individuals become adults. They may have trouble understanding the "hidden curriculum" or unwritten rules of social conduct and effective communication. When rules are understood quite literally it may cause confusion and upset when others disrespect those rules. Understanding deception continues to be a problem for many adults with AS, and they are more likely than typically developing individuals to get involved in financial scams, or to loan money to supposed "friends" who never pay them back. A deficit in understanding what another person knows or does not know can result in providing either too much or too little background information in conversation. Assuming that others possess the same information in their minds as one does oneself can only lead to confusion and miscommunication.

What is important to remember is that in most individuals with ASD the course is one of progress, as long as the individual is motivated and participates actively in appropriate interventions. Once mental health and other important professionals establish a trusting and supportive relationship, their guidance can be invaluable.

Each student is an individual with different needs, but there are several strategies that can be individualized to meet those needs, and that lend themselves quite nicely to developing the skills discussed in Part II. However, creativity has been a key strategy for me in working with my clients. Any of the strategies listed below (as well as others not listed) can be modified to meet a particular individual's needs. I encourage everyone reading this book to use their own creativity in developing or adapting these and other strategies to foster greater awareness and skill development in their clients or students.

- Cognitive Behavioral Therapy (CBT).

- Social Stories™ (Gray 1998).

- Comic Strip Conversations (Gray 1994).

- Emotional Toolbox (Attwood 2007).

- Video modeling.

- Relationship-based therapies.

- Relaxation training and meditation.

- Behavior therapy.

- Role-playing.

- Psycho-education: emotion identification, self-awareness, awareness of others, self-management.

- Self-monitoring (Hume, Loftin and Lantz 2009), especially important in developing independence.

- Visual representation of abstract concepts.

- Visual charts/schedules.

- Bibliotherapy (using books to increase awareness and brainstorm solutions).

- Parent education, partnering with parents as co-therapists at home and in the community.

- Referrals to speech and language pathologists, occupational therapists, educational therapists, and other alternative therapies, as appropriate.

People with ASD have made tremendous contributions to our world since the beginning of time, with minimal intervention. Current intervention programs have enabled many to function at an even higher level. The overriding goal of intervention should be independent functioning in all areas. Toward this end, reliance on adult prompting must be minimized as early as possible. According to Hume *et al.* (2009), numerous intervention strategies successfully target skill acquisition, but "fewer interventions also take into account the development of independent functioning or do so too late after patterns of learning and responding are entrenched" (p.1336).

The following chapters outline in detail various "skill sets" that should enable students to succeed in college, but the overarching principle is to develop independence in all areas as soon as possible. This is true for all students, but students with ASD present with particular challenges that may interfere with their ability and/or willingness to be completely independent. Limitations in executive functioning can make independent functioning difficult overall. Paying particular attention to the individual's degree of ability to tolerate change should guide all intervention goals.

Independent performance of a task, without prompts or stimuli, should be the ultimate goal of any intervention. By striving for as much independent functioning as possible, intervention programs will also succeed in helping people with ASD feel that they are worthwhile, contributing members of society.

PART II
Skill Sets

Introduction

SKILL SETS FOR SUCCESS

BEING "SMART" JUST ISN'T ENOUGH

In the following chapters I will be focusing on developing various skill sets that are important for success in college and beyond. None of the skills in this book have to do with academics. However, they are skills that need to be incorporated into the child's educational programming, as well as the child's intervention outside of school. The sole focus on academics for high functioning (HF) students actually does them a disservice. Students who are "fully included" in general education classes are not typically offered instruction in daily living skills and independence, yet this is the area in which they flounder once they leave high school. Incorporating these skills into the students' overall programming—including their school program—will better prepare them to succeed both academically and independently.

The skill sets presented in the following chapters focus on developing greater self-management and independence. Chapter 2 focuses on self-awareness, which leads to awareness of others. Various aspects of self-awareness will be reviewed prior to moving on to Chapter 3, on environmental skills—knowing how to manage all aspects of one's personal environment and also how to function in multiple environments. Chapter 4 examines the development of self-regulation and self-advocacy—the capacity to understand what one needs, how one functions, and the ability to advocate for oneself in order to acquire the necessary supports to maximize one's ability to learn and adapt. Once these basic skill sets are developed, subsequent skill sets reflect more sophisticated levels of self-management and the capacity to function in a more fluid environment. Chapter 5 deals with organizational skills as pertaining to the environment, learning, and self-monitoring. Executive functioning is also discussed in this chapter. In Chapter 6 the area of asking for help and related skill sets are explored. Self-care skills are discussed in Chapter 7. Finally, social capacities constitute the most sophisticated area of development, and they are examined in Chapter 8, which also includes an overview of Theory of Mind. A summary "Overview of Skill Sets" can be found in the table in Appendix A.

All skill sets are viewed and described from a developmental perspective, because all development occurs in a progression where basic foundational skills form the basis for more sophisticated skills to be fully developed. The concept of a "developmental progression" is applicable to all areas of development including motor, language, social, intellectual, academic and emotional skills. Development also occurs in the context of the environment in which the child lives. Brain development (i.e. "nature") and environmental factors (i.e. "nurture") play a significant role in the maturation process of all individuals. While there are numerous research articles suggesting that the course of development (nature) may be different in the brains of individuals with autistic spectrum disorders (ASD), there is also support in the research literature for early intervention and effective parenting (nurture) as being crucial to the process of potentially re-programming neural circuits.

This means that intervention designed to foster the development of these skill sets needs to begin at the time the child is first diagnosed, if not before. However, most families of children with ASD don't know that their child has a developmental disability for several years, with the average child being diagnosed at approximately seven to nine years of age (Klin, Volkmar and Sparrow 2000). By this time they may have settled into a routine that feels comfortable. Changing well-established routines can be difficult for students with ASD, and gaining the child's willingness to begin getting involved in his own self-care may be challenging.

The student's full participation can be difficult to attain for other reasons as well. First, many skills are difficult to learn, retain, and generalize into various settings. Second, some students cannot understand why they need to learn particular skill sets, and/or resist learning them because the skill is not a preferred activity. Their resistance can be intense, and for many parents it may feel simpler (and certainly less stressful) to forgo the battle. Therefore, we must find ways to support parents so that they do not take the route of allowing their child to be dependent. In so doing we can help parents foster a family culture that values, encourages, and reinforces independence and becomes incorporated into the student's (and the family's) daily routine, building on early foundational skills to develop more sophisticated skills over time.

Coordination between the family and other service providers will be essential. I frequently adopt a case management approach by taking the lead in interfacing with, and coordinating services between, the child's support team, the family, and the various recommendations I make for the child's progress. There are numerous ways to do this, and families are very appreciative of my willingness to engage in this process.

Children with ASD will benefit greatly if all providers of intervention can find ways to incorporate the development of these skills into their respective treatment plans. Because generalization of learning is difficult for individuals with ASD, opportunities to practice these skills in all environments—home, community, and school—will help students feel better prepared, and make the transition to post-secondary education (PSE) less stressful.

Each of the following chapters identifies specific skills in a broader area of functioning (self-awareness, self-help, etc.). A rationale for why students need the particular skill is offered, as is an explanation of how the skill contributes to a successful PSE experience. While some sections detail suggestions for "early" and "later" preparation, others may not make these distinctions, for reasons that should be obvious to the reader. "Early preparation" relates to the early developmental trajectory from the time of diagnosis through the beginning of middle school. "Later preparation" relates to the later middle school and the high-school years. It's important to remember that these intervention periods are recommendations and that individual differences in each student must be taken into consideration. Although this is not a curriculum *per se*, I do provide examples of possible interventions in each section. My hope is that professionals reading this manual will exercise their own creativity in collaboration with the members of the student's treatment team and the parents, in order to develop the most appropriate, individualized interventions for their particular student.

Most of the skill sets in these chapters are *prerequisite* to success in college and beyond. However, some skill sets will need to be learned in the college environment. These are interspersed throughout the skill sets of Part II, and are also discussed in Part III. All students will be better off if parents, teachers, school districts, state disability agencies, and all other professionals who work with them, work together to promote development of the skills and tools they will need to succeed in life, whether they decide to pursue PSE or any other type of training.

A note to readers: In the following chapters I make reference to "many" or "most" individuals with ASD, although I am keenly aware that there is great variability in skill level among individuals with ASD. Also, "student/students" or "individual/individuals" in this text refers to students or people with ASD. Finally, "college" will be used as the generic term for all PSE institutions.

Chapter 2

SELF-AWARENESS
SKILL SETS

Psychologically, self-awareness is key in the development of "self" because it is the precursor to awareness of others. Without knowing oneself and how to identify various aspects and characteristics of oneself, it will be next to impossible to identify those same characteristics in others. While typically developing children develop these abilities without direct instruction, individuals with autistic spectrum disorders (ASD) will need to "learn" in a more structured, didactic manner. Psychologists who have extensive training and experience in working with individuals with ASD will provide a somewhat modified version of Cognitive Behavioral Therapy and psycho-education (Attwood 2007) to foster self-awareness, awareness of others, and reciprocity. Development in this area is crucial for a well-rounded individual, but unfortunately it is often missed for a number of reasons.

The importance of self-awareness in the development of children and adults with ASD is grossly under-emphasized in the literature and in the educational programming of students. I believe this occurs because self-awareness falls more into the "psychological" than the educational realm. Furthermore, the need for psychological assistance of any kind continues to be stigmatized in many cultures, which usually delays onset of treatment well beyond the initial need. Although many parents of individuals with ASD realize that their child would benefit from working with a therapist, their decision to seek out a trained professional may be thwarted by the disapproval they expect that they will face from other family members and friends. Parents of children with ASD also struggle with ongoing familial and societal blame suggesting that parenting skills are at the root of their child's problems, and so they often avoid seeking therapy for their child out of fear that the child's problems are, in fact, due to their own shortcomings (Freedman 2001).

Issues of the "self" and of an emotional nature tend to be dismissed or under-valued in many cultures. Often the need for assistance in this area is thought to be shameful. Nevertheless, some authors refer to self-awareness as "the pinnacle of mental functioning" (Perry 2009). Self-awareness involves "knowing what we are thinking and feeling while we think and feel and perceive, and while our thoughts and feelings and perceptions change right before our eyes" (Perry 2009, p.96). Knowing leads to informed decision-making and action. Without self-awareness, "acting upon those thoughts, feelings, and perceptions, both automatically and by deliberation, and moving between the automatic and the deliberate with recognition of that movement" (Perry 2009, p.96), is next to impossible. For most of us, these functions develop over time as we mature and piece the various experiences of our lives together to make meaning. We use that information to determine future decisions, attitudes, and morals. Because of their brain differences, these functions do not develop naturally or automatically in individuals with ASD. They need highly specific, focused, and sophisticated intervention in order to compensate for these differences.

As mentioned above, school districts and state disability agencies place little, if any, emphasis on these areas, except for providing occasional intervention to develop "social skills." I believe this reflects a lack of awareness of (and possibly training in) the types of psychologically based skills that individuals with ASD need in order to assimilate effectively into society. Parents also place a great deal of emphasis on academics, in large part because academics are important and are usually an area of strength in their child. Furthermore, academic skills are tangible and parents can track progress and provide assistance in this area. The idea that a person might need to "learn" how to understand and do something that most of us pick up without direct instruction is difficult to grasp. Teaching something as abstract and limitless as learning how to read nonverbal cues, or how to understand others' minds, becomes a challenge in and of itself.

Self-awareness is multi-dimensional and abstract. There are various components and it is important to help students develop abilities in all of them. These skill sets should be a part of the student's intervention program from the beginning, and they need to be delivered in developmentally appropriate stages. For example, a preschool child begins to understand the significance of the four basic emotions: happy, sad, mad, and scared. As the child matures, she experiences more sophisticated emotions (e.g. frustration, jealousy) and learns how to recognize and deal with combinations of emotions. Be aware that increasing individuals' capacity for self-awareness can trigger depression and/or anxiety in people with ASD as a result of the heightened awareness of the challenges they face. Parents, clinicians and other professionals involved with the student must always be on the lookout for symptoms of depression or anxiety so that an appropriate referral for treatment can be made.

The rest of this chapter will focus on the various aspects of self-awareness.

SELF-ACCEPTANCE

Usually students with ASD who succeed in college will also demonstrate a willingness to understand and accept their differences, including:

- acceptance of their disability and learning differences (this doesn't mean they like it, but they accept it)
- willingness to disclose their disability/challenges to, and to work closely with, advisors and professors
- interest in learning more about what kind of assistance they will need
- willingness to ask for as much help as they need in order to succeed

- willingness to work closely with the college's Disabilities Services Office.

We all have individual differences regardless of whether we have a disability or not, and accepting our unique profile of abilities and challenges enables us to seek out assistance and maximize our learning. Limitations in self-awareness make it difficult for individuals with ASD to understand and accept their many strengths and weaknesses. The first step towards change is acceptance that a problem or deficit exists. The next step is being willing to work towards making a change. Without self-awareness and self-acceptance, students will most likely be resistant to addressing areas of need and further developing themselves.

Without self-acceptance, students will also resist asking for accommodations that would otherwise help them succeed in college and in the workplace. Many students resist getting help from the Disabilities Services Office (DSO) because they don't fully understand what types of services are offered. Coulter (2003, p.1) writes that her son "thought that 'academic resource center' meant psychological counseling so he refused to go for help." Other students refuse to avail themselves of these services because of the word "disabilities." Coulter also notes that many students with ASD are simply tired of being labeled as a "special education student." They don't want to be known as a student who needs additional assistance, they want to be "normal." Many students see going to college as a way of getting away from special education and from their parents' involvement in their schooling. The students that I've worked with also resist asking for accommodations because they feel that it is equivalent to cheating or getting benefits that others don't get. What all students with disabilities need to understand is that "…accommodations are intended to level the playing field by removing barriers" and enabling students with disabilities to "have an equal opportunity to access the programs, activities, and services of the college… Accommodations provide a fair chance for students who are otherwise qualified; they do not provide an unfair advantage" (Johnson and Hines 2005, p.42). Students sometimes also struggle to understand why they need accommodations because they know they're "smart." This often leads to feelings of inadequacy and thoughts like, "If I would try harder…spend more time…focus better…[etc.], I could do it without extra help."

We know that positive reinforcement is essential to helping students feel good about themselves in general, but getting students to understand and accept the limitations and strengths that spring from their constitutional, temperamental, or genetic makeup is not something most educators are trained to do. Lack of training is one of many roadblocks to facilitating greater self-awareness in individuals with ASD. Other related roadblocks include a paucity of well-trained diagnosticians and the unfortunate experience of receiving multiple misdiagnoses over the course of the individual's life. Parents' confusion over telling their child about their diagnosis can also play a part in limiting self-awareness and self-acceptance.

Many parents hesitate to tell their child that he or she has an autism spectrum disorder. Understandably, some parents don't like the idea of "labeling" (aka "diagnosing") their child, and feel that individual differences should be accepted and embraced. In an ideal world this is true, and is the way it "should" be. However, in the world as it is today, it's not always so. Currently, a label or diagnosis may be the only way for a child to receive specialized services or accommodations. It is a harsh reality that government agencies and state education departments in the United States have varying, but usually limited, funds. One of the ways they choose to manage their funds is to provide services to those who really need them. Diagnosis is one way to differentiate between the various types of issues students have, and schools and agencies use diagnosis as a preliminary indication of the level of care and/or assistance that a student may need. Students who need accommodations in the PSE setting will not get them without a formal diagnosis. Therefore, it's possible that choosing not to tell individuals (at the right time and in the correct manner) about their ASD may actually hurt them in the long run. Once students are out of high school, there are fewer laws that protect their educational rights. Therefore, students need to be able to advocate for themselves in order to receive specific accommodations in the PSE setting. (See Chapter 4 for further discussion.)

When parents struggle with this issue it is important for the clinician to help them identify personal conflicts and feelings in order to make a more objective decision after disclosure. Parents naturally feel a tremendous sadness about diagnosis of their child's disability. They are concerned that their child will be stigmatized or ostracized, especially because so many people either don't know enough about ASD or will have negative associations with the word "autism." These are real concerns because there are many occasions when individuals are shunned because of their differences. Parents are also concerned that if their child "knows" she is different as a result of being told that she has ASD, it will have a negative impact on the child's self-esteem. This assumes that the child is unaware of being different, or that if she is aware, this has not affected the child's self-esteem. Unfortunately, this is not the case in reality. Any student who *is* different is aware of being different, whether she talks about it or not.

What I have learned from my clients is that when individuals do not know what makes them different, they develop multiple, negative impressions or fantasies about themselves. Furthermore, because no one is talking about their differences or why they are different, they come to the conclusion that it's a big secret that no one wants to talk about. This then leads to increased feelings of isolation. In my clinical practice and the practices of all of my colleagues who work with this population, recently diagnosed adult clients have disclosed that before they knew about their diagnoses they believed that they were crazy, retarded, psychotic, and numerous other extremely negative descriptors. Knowledge is power, and learning about their diagnosis enabled them to read about it, identify with a group of other people like themselves, and experience a degree of hope for improvement through treatment. A recent news article reported on a brilliant 50-year-old man with two advanced degrees, who struggled to maintain a job and ended up working as a janitor. This man shared that he had had feelings of worthlessness for most of his life until he was diagnosed with Asperger's syndrome (AS). The diagnosis gave him some answers and enabled him to realize his worth and his talents. Like many others in his situation, he has found satisfaction and hope in educating people in his community about AS (Safos 2008). For Liane Willey, getting a diagnosis of AS was a life-altering experience. She notes that she "was able to seek out the right kind of treatment, and after a lifetime of mimicking others, finally find my own identity" (Interlandi 2008, p.4).

I've learned a great deal about this issue from adults that I've worked with who were not diagnosed as youngsters. Here are some of their insights into the issue of knowing vs. not knowing about their disability.

- Knowing about their disability helps people to feel as if they're not crazy after all.

- Knowing about their disability helps people feel as if they belong to a group of other individuals who are like them.

- Knowing about their disability has helped many individuals with ASD feel proud of who they are.

- Knowing about their disability helps people plan their lives in a realistic manner, both in terms of future career planning and family planning.

- Knowing about their disability helps people understand themselves and move towards greater self-acceptance and less self-blame.

- Knowing about their disability helps people advocate for themselves and talk about their strengths and challenges so that others can understand and accept them.

- Knowing they have an autism spectrum disorder gives people an opportunity to look up to their own role models—Temple Grandin, Stephen Shore, Jerry Newport, Thomas Jefferson, Albert Einstein, or other individuals with known or suspected ASD.

- Knowing they have an autism spectrum disorder enables people to find others who are like them and receive mentoring from them.

- From a genetic standpoint, individuals with ASD have a right to know.

Another roadblock to self-acceptance is the "invisible" nature of ASD in most "high functioning" (HF) individuals. The profile of strengths and weaknesses is also highly inconsistent from individual to individual, and there often isn't one single, identifiable "look" or behavior pattern that is consistently seen in all individuals with ASD. This makes it very difficult for some parents and families to accept that their child has a disability of any kind. In the child's early years most parents of individuals later diagnosed with ASD believed that they had a "normal" child. Making the transition can be very difficult and is a process that parents must go through at their own pace. Even once the diagnosis is made and accepted, parents often talk about how at times their child is "right on," can answer questions, follow directions, etc., while at other times the child's responsiveness is surprisingly limited. Parents see those "right on" moments as glimmers of hope that their child is, in fact, "normal." Unfortunately, inconsistency is the most consistent feature of ASD.

The many roadblocks to acceptance for families of individuals with ASD can, in turn, complicate the process of self-acceptance for the individual. However, one way that parents can help their child with acceptance is to model tolerance for differences in all individuals throughout the child's life. Parents can help their child reflect on and remember their positive attributes. Children need to learn that they are not defined by having ASD and that in some ways they possess strengths that others do not have, as a result of having ASD. Nick Dubin (2005) is a man with ASD who writes about the areas in which he struggles as a result of ASD, but also considers himself to be blessed in a number of ways. He refers to himself as "an original thinker, a very focused individual, a nonconformist, an intelligent person, compassionate, reflected (introverted), honest (pathologically so)" (p.102). The child's strengths and weaknesses can be openly discussed within the context of the family. Ultimately, the child's acceptance of who he is, ASD and all, hinges on the parents' acceptance. As professionals, it is our job to facilitate this process for the parents of our clients, so that they, in turn, can facilitate the process in their own child.

As professionals we cannot underestimate the human desire to belong and feel that one's differences are not so great as to set them apart from everyone else—the need to fit in is a normal part of development. Everyone who, for whatever reason, doesn't fit in experiences an ongoing mourning process related to feeling "different." These feelings come and go throughout the individual's life, in varying degrees at different times. I've found this process to be especially powerful in individuals who have "invisible" disabilities such as ASD, epilepsy, or learning disabilities. It's almost as if they carry this "secret" that no one can see or suspects, yet they very much know it's there and that it sets them apart from others. Professionals who work with individuals with disabilities must be sensitive and willing to address this with their clients.

RECOGNITION OF PHYSICAL AND EMOTIONAL STATES

The first and most important step in self-awareness is developing an awareness of one's own physical and emotional states of being. This is a developmental process that, in typical development, begins in infancy and continues throughout the lifespan. Physical states such as hunger, cold, hot, thirst, fatigue, etc., may be easier to identify than emotional states, although many students surprisingly need help in this area.

The developmental track for individuals with ASD may be different when it comes to emotions, and individual differences in this area need to be identified. Ultimately, there may be some individuals with ASD who will remain confused when it comes to emotions. Temple Grandin (Grandin and Barron 2005) alludes to this, noting that an individual with ASD "may derive greater happiness through work or hobbies than through pure emotional bonding" (p.46). However, it is still important to provide education and support in the early years so that, at minimum, basic emotional awareness can be achieved. In addition to basic self-awareness, Mayer, Salovey and Caruso (2008) note that higher level emotional awareness skills include "the capacity to manage emotions properly...(a) perceive emotions in oneself and others accurately, (b) use the emotions to facilitate thinking, (c) understand emotions, emotional language, and the signals conveyed by emotions, and (d) manage emotions so as to attain specific goals" (p.506).

Early preparation

When a young student appears not to have a grasp on physical states (hunger, cold, hot, thirst, fatigue, etc.), a consultation with a neurologist is warranted. Once any neurological causes are ruled out, sensory disturbances must be considered and an evaluation by an occupational therapist is warranted. There are many strategies that can facilitate greater understanding of the physical cues our bodies give us. In very young children parents can facilitate this kind of learning by verbalizing their observations about the child's needs ("Your tummy is growling... you must be hungry"). Social Stories™ (Gray 1998) are also useful in helping elementary-aged students connect bodily cues with physical needs. This skill needs to be in place by the time the student enters middle school.

As mentioned above, individuals with ASD will need ongoing support in recognizing their own emotions, beginning from rudimentary emotions such as happy, sad, mad, scared, to the ever increasing complexity of emotions that evolve throughout the lifespan. Most parenting classes for parents of typically developing children emphasize the importance of providing children with an emotional lexicon. Once children are diagnosed with ASD, all of the professionals on the support treatment team will be instrumental in helping them develop physical and emotional awareness. As part of the student's intervention team it's important for professionals (and parents) to insist that the team focus on developing emotional awareness. I emphasize this because, unfortunately, this is an area that is often overlooked by school districts whose primary focus is academics. However, the ability to remain physically *and* emotionally regulated is prerequisite for learning. If children are unable to identify their physical and emotional states they won't be able to learn, regulate themselves, and develop adaptive coping strategies. Depending on the level of sophistication of the treatment team, it may also be necessary for the treatment team to be trained in how to foster physical and emotional awareness in the students they work with. Because emotional awareness is traditionally not considered to be part of a standard educational curriculum, this idea may meet with some resistance. School districts provide reading accommodations and special instruction for students who struggle with reading, ranging from books on tape to Braille for blind students—but a student with ASD needs special instruction in learning to "read" emotions, first in themselves and then in others. Without this skill it will be impossible for the student to understand subtle looks or verbal cues from teachers or peers, making it difficult for them to truly benefit from, and progress in, their educational program.

Later preparation

Older students can be taught to recognize the physiological, behavioral, and environmental clues that something may be amiss within themselves. It is essential that they learn, practice, and become good evaluators of their own physical and emotional well-being. The student's particular learning or processing challenges can compound the frequency and intensity of experiencing these uncomfortable emotional states, but students who can recognize the signs that they are upset will find it easier to manage their reactions. In addition to depression, a significant number of individuals with ASD are prone to anxiety, in part as a result of not fully understanding others or the world they live in. According to Harpur, Lawlor and Fitzgerald (2004, p.213), students with ASD can experience panic attacks when faced with "stressful events such as not knowing what to do in a situation, being ridiculed by others, misunderstanding a social context, relationship breakdown, disappointments, the death of someone supportive, and other stressful incidents."

The following strategies can be useful to enhance the student's understanding of confusing social situations: Comic Strip Conversations (Gray 1998), Social Stories™ (Gray 1998), video modeling and role-playing. Learning to recognize anxiety and depression enables students to learn strategies to manage these feelings and/or learn who to go to for assistance when what they've tried hasn't worked. Psycho-education and Cognitive Behavioral Therapy (CBT) are both extremely useful strategies for increasing self-awareness and self-management.

In the college setting, awareness of one's emotions becomes crucial, particularly awareness of the symptoms of depression and anxiety. In their study of depressive symptoms in adults with ASD, Sterling et al. (2008) noted that high functioning individuals endorsed more symptoms of depression. Along with higher cognitive abilities comes greater awareness of one's shortcomings. Higher functioning individuals may also be exposed to and expected to cope with more sophisticated and challenging social situations. Their higher cognitive abilities can be deceptive to others and so lead to higher expectations, often resulting in the individual's perception that he has failed to meet these expectations. The authors also note that "Repeated rejection coupled with lack of understanding, insight, or skills needed to modify strategies, could certainly lead to the development of depressive symptoms" (p.1016). Finally, it's not uncommon for individuals with ASD to exhibit other co-morbid psychiatric symptoms. Individuals who learn to identify and develop strategies to deal with their emotions feel a sense of pride, success and internal resourcefulness that they can depend on in all aspects of their lives.

SELF-REGULATION/EMOTION MANAGEMENT

Once students recognize they're in a critical physical or emotional state, they need tools to deal with their emotions and reactions. Tony Attwood (2007) developed the concept of an "emotional toolbox" where students learn cognitive restructuring and develop a set of tools or strategies to use when dealing with various emotional reactions. These can be physical tools, relaxation tools, social tools, thinking tools, and special interest tools, designed to enhance the student's ability to manage his emotions. The tools are developed together with the student and are visually represented on a card that he uses as a cue at the appropriate time in any environment. Although this strategy may sound simplistic to some, it is actually quite sophisticated and is suitable for use with individuals of all ages, not to mention those with a range of developmental and psychiatric problems. Once skills are developed, students learn to use the tools in their toolboxes effectively.

Early preparation

When working with younger children the primary focus will be on awareness of their own basic emotions and physical states. The four basic feelings are: happy, sad, mad, and scared. Psycho-education is used to introduce the concept of emotions, and enable students to identify emotions in pictures and video, in themselves and ultimately in other people in their immediate families. *In vivo* learning, as well as learning from books, about emotions and activities that enhance awareness of emotions is most effective. With maturity, children should learn to identify emotions in immediate family members and then in their friends. Learning then takes the form of identifying the effect that others' behavior has on them and the effect that their behavior has on others. The child's likes and dislikes should be verbalized and discussed in multiple environments. The child should also learn about the likes and dislikes of other familiar people. Basic characteristics should be taught, including physical attributes (e.g. brown hair, blue eyes, tall, short, etc.) and personal attributes (e.g. nice, friendly, giving). From there, students move into higher levels of character development.

Later preparation

Once the fundamental four emotions have been learned and integrated, older students can begin to learn about more sophisticated and abstract emotions, such as frustration, disappointment, loss, jealousy, embarrassment, etc. They also need to learn how their emotions affect others, and how others' emotions affect them. The emotional toolbox strategy (Attwood 2007) can be expanded when working with older teens and adults with (and without) ASD, because the strategies they might choose to use will be more sophisticated than those of younger children. Also, the toolbox concept offers a concrete "tool" to help deal with more abstract emotions. Older students can also learn to be more independent in this process, although at times they may still need cuing from others around them. Once students recognize their emotional state, they can turn to the various "tools" in their toolbox to help manage the emotion and identify solutions to problem situations more independently.

For both young and older learners, it's important not to assume that once a tool has been mastered, the student will automatically apply it in other similar situations—transfer of skills and strategies learned in one setting to another setting is a particular problem in ASD. Therefore, ongoing practice in a variety of situations will be needed. It will also be helpful to role-play hypothetical problem situations and have the student select the most appropriate tool for that situation. Even this type of practice can be difficult for many students and it may be necessary for students to have ongoing contact with their therapist until there is sufficient evidence that they are spontaneously applying strategies and tools to various different situations. The types of professionals who can help students in this area include psychologists, marriage and family therapists, social workers, educational therapists, speech and language therapists, school counselors, school psychologists, teachers, and any other professionals who possess the necessary experience and training in ASD. However, I've also seen very talented and gifted high-school and college students with an intuitive knack for working with students with ASD be very successful mentors in this area.

LEARNING AND PRACTICING STRESS MANAGEMENT TECHNIQUES

Learning and practicing stress management techniques is essential to the successful management of our emotions. Many of us naturally turn to our hobbies or other activities that we find relaxing when we feel stressed. However, people who experience high levels of anxiety may find more formal approaches, such as meditation, yoga, or deep breathing, more effective. For students with ASD, stress levels can be compounded by sensory issues. Therefore, a key aspect in the student's program should include a sensory integration evaluation to determine the role that sensory issues play in elevating the student's stress level. If that role is found to be significant, occupational therapy (OT) will be a key component of the student's intervention program. Parents should note that school-based OT is very different from clinic-based OT. School-based OT primarily focuses on the kind of intervention a student needs to benefit from schooling, and typically involves activities to strengthen the student's writing abilities. Clinic-based OT focuses more on the whole student, treating all aspects of the student's sensory deficits or needs. Often school districts will not cover the costs of clinic-based OT, and parents may have to pay out of pocket or go through their private insurance plans.

Students with ASD will more readily understand and accept the benefits of relaxation and stress management techniques when these are explained scientifically and physiologically to them. The idea that our nervous system cannot simultaneously be in both a stressed and a relaxed state resonates with most people—even young people with ASD. If necessary, therapists can show the student developmentally appropriate literature that describes the benefits of relaxation, meditation, and other types of stress management techniques. Students who have problems with sensory integration can learn to use specific activities to stay calm or alert.

The challenging part often comes in getting students to practice these techniques consistently at home. They need to know that by practicing stress reduction when they are not stressed out, they learn how to induce a state of relaxation when they *are* stressed out. This enables them to engage stress reduction readily, so that they can handle stressful situations with a level head. Toward this end, it is essential to get the family involved, as it is the parents and other members of the student's support team who will be following through with practice in the home setting. If relaxation and stress management become part of the family culture, students will have an easier time incorporating them when needed.

Early preparation

Learning to identify one's emotions will be critical for early learners. Teaching strategies such as seeking out comfort when sad or hurt, pounding a pillow or jumping on a trampoline to let off steam, turning to their favorite pet or book, etc., will help with early stress management. Some children may benefit from implementing a "sensory diet" in school and other settings. This term applies to various accommodations or modifications that can be made to help the child remain regulated in the school environment. Some examples of these strategies include: sitting on a small inflatable cushion, frequent breaks, taking tests in a quiet room, having a "fidget item" for the student at her desk, etc. Students also benefit greatly from parents narrating their own stress management strategies while modeling them ("I'm so frustrated right now, I think I'm going to go for a walk/jump on the trampoline/sit in a quiet room for a few minutes"). When children with ASD begin the process of learning formal relaxation strategies to help them with self-regulation and emotion management by at least the third grade, there is a greater chance that they will incorporate this practice into their daily routine as young adults.

Later preparation

Assuming stress management is a part of the student's family culture, ongoing practice and learning more sophisticated strategies, including relaxation training, yoga and/or meditation, is essential. Students should become increasingly independent in determining and implementing various strategies before they graduate from high school. The ability to regulate oneself is crucial for survival in college. Dorm living can present sensory overload for many students, and there are various sensory challenges inherent in the classroom. These considerations will be discussed further in Part III.

LINKING AND RETRIEVING PERSONAL, EMOTIONAL EVENTS

The ability of individuals with ASD to make links between their experiences and their emotions may be affected in ways that have not been highly studied. Challenges in this area may, in part, help to explain why it is so difficult for some individuals with ASD to provide a coherent, sequential narrative of their experiences with sufficient context for the listener truly to understand and relate to their experience. It may also contribute to the way personal and emotional experiences are stored in their memories. According to Crane and Goddard (2008), adults with ASD demonstrated a deficit in "personal episodic memory," as well as "evidence of a deficit dissociation between personal episodic and personal semantic memory" (p.505). In their study, the control group of matched, typically developing adults was able to use their memories of "secondary school and the five years post school time periods" to enhance autobiographical memories, while the ASD group did not. The authors note the following:

> Considering the importance of the adolescence and early adult life time periods in the formation of both self and social identity, this has important implications regarding the social difficulties experienced in ASD. Future research is therefore necessary to explore these memory difficulties in greater depth and to identify the mechanisms underlying the episodic autobiographical memory difficulties in ASD. (p.505)

This is an important developmental piece of information and absent evidence-based interventions, there are some preliminary strategies that families, schools, and other agencies interfacing with the student can use to facilitate development of this very important function.

Early preparation

From very early on in the student's development, parents should be encouraged to review the student's daily experiences, remembering to incorporate the feelings and perspectives of the student and others with whom he has interacted. Especially with young children, but even with older students, this process is even more powerful when daily experiences can be given visual representation. So, for example, it's handy to carry a digital camera and take pictures of the child engaging in various activities. These pictures can be used to create a short story about the student's day. I realize that this can be a monumental task to expect of parents, and it is not necessary to provide a visual image of the entire day, every day. The intention would be that, by providing the child with this type of activity in multiple environments over the course of time, memory processes will be stimulated and reinforced. Social Stories™ (Gray 1998) can also be very useful for remembering experiences and making emotional links.

Later preparation

I encourage parents to keep up the above practice until their child refuses to continue any longer. Writing notes on the backs of photographs can also help. I encourage parents to engage the student in looking at photographs of their lives on a regular basis. When asking a student about her day, it will be important to incorporate questions about her own reactions to and perceptions of the situation, as well as the reactions and perceptions of others involved. Older students might want to keep a diary, although challenges associated with writing may deter some. If so, students can be offered the opportunity to dictate to a parent or another adult, and when they are old enough they can use dictation software for this purpose. Older students should be allowed a modicum of privacy for their diaries. However, for this particular purpose it will be important to have a parent or other trained interventionist (teacher, therapist, coach, etc.) facilitate the process to ensure that the student taps into the personal and emotional aspects of the experience. Many students with ASD may miss these important factors and simply report on the concrete things they did throughout their day. Finally, Social Stories™ (Gray 1998) can be very useful for older students as well.

RECOGNIZING THE IMPORTANCE OF GETTING PSYCHOLOGICAL SUPPORT, AND KNOWING WHEN, WHERE, AND FROM WHOM TO SEEK IT

Once students are able to recognize their various emotional states and practice self-regulation, it becomes easier for them to know when to ask for help—when whatever they've tried doesn't work, or if they continue to feel distressed, depressed, or anxious.

Early preparation

Most parents provide their young children with information about what to do if they get lost, if they need help, if a stranger approaches them, etc. However, children with ASD will actually need practice with this, and I recommend that parents and other interventionists practice this skill with them in multiple environments. Children can learn to ask others for assistance when at the mall, grocery store, etc. Note that because of inherent communication problems in ASD, this may be a difficult skill to attain. However, practicing it is essential.

Later preparation

This type of learning needs to continue as long as students are living at home. All being well, by the time they go to college, they will recognize the importance of getting help. In the college setting students will need to be prepared with information on where and from whom to get support on and off campus. This information should be secured in advance of the student's attendance at college. Students need to know where campus health services are. They also need to know how to contact health services and/or the school's counseling center. They should identify and keep a written record of the hours of operation for each of these, so that they can plan when to make contact. Hotline numbers should also be provided in case a student needs assistance during off hours. Many students do not want to avail themselves of campus counseling services, for a number of reasons. Some fear being seen by their peers at the counseling office. Some may want to keep their "issues" separate from the college. Some may carry a negative association with college counseling services because of experiences they may have had at their high school's counseling office. Therefore, we cannot assume that just providing students with various resources means that they will use them. This is an area that needs pre-emptive exploration and clarification, so that parents and college advisors are sure that students accept the type of assistance being offered, and if not, alternative plans can be made.

If the family elects to have a private mental health practitioner off campus, the student should have met with that person at least once before school starts, and should have that person's number handy in either his electronic or paper collection of phone numbers. It is very important for parents and students to find out whether anyone working for campus counseling services has experience working with individuals with ASD. If not, I strongly urge finding a clinician in the community who does. Working with individuals with ASD is a specialty area that requires specific training and experience, and not all psychologists, mental health workers, or psychiatrists have the background to treat ASD effectively. A particular clinician may be very highly thought of in the community, but if he or she does not have the proper training and experience, it is likely that treatment will be ineffective and the student will be averse to continuing in treatment with anyone else. This makes sense if we think about seeking medical treatment in general—if you have a specific medical problem, you want to see a specialist in that area. Similarly, if you have specific psychological needs, you want to be certain that the clinician is capable of treating you. According to the American Psychological Association, mental health practitioners are supposed to practice within their area of competence. For clients with issues for which a clinician has no training and experience, an appropriate referral is supposed to be made if the practitioner cannot secure ample consultation to treat the client. However, buyer beware… not all practitioners do this. Therefore, it is appropriate, as the "consumer" of services, to ask detailed questions about the practitioner's training in the area of ASD before engaging them for treatment. The best way to get a good referral in a new town is to ask the Disabilities Services Office, or to contact the local Autism Society.

Chapter 3

ENVIRONMENTAL SKILL SETS

The two broad areas dealt with in this chapter concern skills that enable students to develop increasing independence in managing their environments, their routines, and their own reactions to the external world. Once again, the sooner these skills become a part of the student's repertoire, the more likely it is that he or she will become completely independent. The best way to foster the development of these skills is to provide opportunities for students to complete these tasks in the natural course of their daily lives, and continually provide them with specific strategies and feedback about their performance.

CREATING SAMENESS AND ESTABLISHING ROUTINES (WHILE REMAINING FLEXIBLE!)

Individuals with autistic spectrum disorders (ASD) thrive on sameness and need a sense of sameness in order to feel safe and organized. Although students may have developed routines at home, these routines may be ineffective in the college setting, due to the subtle and not-so-subtle differences between home and school. New routines will have to be developed in practically all areas: when, where, and how the student completes homework, fixes or purchases meals, takes medication, gets money, etc. It's important to remember that, when entering new environments, students with ASD may not be able to fluidly and independently adapt their previous routines and practices to the new situation.

Early preparation

People with ASD may not realize early on that there are numerous routines that they engage in throughout their day. I usually ask my clients to tell me their bedtime or bathing routines and, in spite of being highly verbal, many of them cannot. As I probe further to determine whether they're struggling because of verbal or sequencing issues, in many cases it becomes evident that the child simply has not paid attention to the fact that he or she typically does certain things in a specific sequence. Yet the same child may be unable to tolerate taking a different route to a familiar location! The main point here is that when a routine is important to a child with ASD, it *must* be adhered to Otherwise the child may not be picking up on (or paying attention to) things that happen routinely on a daily basis.

Routines are related to sequencing, which is a very important learning concept. Parents and educators can quite easily make the child aware of various routines throughout the day. I recommend doing so verbally and, most important, visually, because people with ASD seem to respond more readily to visual than to auditory input. Making a visual representation of the steps to a particular routine will help the child remember them better. This often has the added benefit of helping children to become more independent and need less "nagging" to complete their routines.

There are many common daily routines to consider. Most families have a morning or getting-ready-for-school routine. It's very helpful to establish a routine for getting dressed in the morning. Usually when children get home from school there's a routine that includes doing homework. Most families have a bedtime routine. When children experience anxiety or impulsivity, I also help them develop their own routines or rituals to help manage these potentially disruptive internal experiences.

If we think about our lives, much of what we do has a specific pattern that may vary from time to time, but predictability helps us get through the day, knowing what needs to be done and what to anticipate next. Once children understand the importance and existence of routines, they then need to learn to problem-solve situations where they cannot follow their typical routines. At school there are many opportunities for the child to learn how to cope with interruptions to routines— having a substitute teacher; assemblies that interrupt the daily classroom structure, or lunch/recess routines, etc. I often "mix things up" during sessions, and likewise encourage parents to introduce changes as often as possible at home. A calendar is an effective tool here. The student's daily activities can be charted on the calendar, and whenever changes occur they can be incorporated into the visual schedule of activities. Sometimes changes are unpredictable, and the calendar can be used in these instances too, by making the change on it afterwards and engaging the child in a discussion about how he handled the disruption.

The process of adjusting and then problem-solving changes in routines may need to happen very gradually for some children, but it does need to happen. The other key point is that the child needs to be included in the problem-solving process when a particular routine cannot be completed. Helping children understand and remember routines and learn to problem-solve when their routines have to change will go a long way towards teaching them to be independent and self-reliant adults.

Later preparation

All of the preceding suggestions should be implemented throughout the student's day in multiple environments and should always be included in the student's educational programming, even in the later school years. Older children should learn to use a planner. It enables them to remember their homework and eventually can be used as a tool to assist them in breaking down their work into manageable chunks. Planners can also be used for organization and time management. I often tell my clients that in my experience the most common predictor of success in college is whether or not a student uses a planner. Students who use their planners effectively are more likely to succeed than students who do not. I've had a great deal of success in engaging "planner-resistant" students by using this anecdotal bit of information.

Because routines help students with ASD be more consistent in following through on things, it is important to help them establish routines for doing their laundry, personal hygiene, reconciling their bank accounts, and other activities that don't take place every day but need to be taken care of within the month. I recommend establishing a laundry day each week, and a schedule for personal hygiene, such as shaving or washing one's hair either daily or every other day—and then sticking to the schedule as much as possible. If routines such as these can be established while students are still living at home, they will feel like successful, contributing members of their family, while simultaneously developing excellent coping strategies for independent living.

Not all changes can be anticipated, but there are some areas in which I recommend that students get specific input to help manage particular routines once they leave home. It is especially important to consider this in the area of safety and well-being. The issue of medication comes to mind here. Usually by the time students are in high school they have a fairly predictable routine for taking daily medication (for example). However, I have worked with several clients who were unable to make the necessary modifications to their medication regimen after they left home for college. In some cases the results could have been extremely dangerous. Therefore, when it comes to medical issues I recommend that students have regular contact with their parents for a designated period of time. One way to accomplish this is for the student to sign a Health Insurance Portability and Accountability Act (HIPAA) release so that parents can continue to participate in the student's medical care to some degree (Trudeau 2008). HIPAA is among the most recent of medical privacy laws enacted in the United States to protect patient confidentiality. It offers patients the right to specifically deny or assign access to their medical records. Without specific assignment, medical records can only be made available to the patient/individual. By assigning access to a parent(s), even temporarily, the student's health and well-being is protected until the student is able to manage these affairs independently. Incidentally, I encourage *all* students to consider this option, not just students with ASD.

Ensuring the student's safety and well-being within the classroom environment is also essential to a successful PSE experience. Some students may feel more comfortable when they sit in the same seat for each class. This can usually be worked out with the professor in advance. Other students "may need to carry 'odd' objects to class and around campus with them. This is a way to feel anchored and should not be discouraged" (Prince-Hughes 2002, p.125). There are numerous other examples of the need for sameness and routine in individuals with ASD. In fact, most of us function best when we have some sort of predictability in our lives and it is important to respect the student's needs in this area in order to facilitate greater independence, generalization and problem-solving. Ultimately, the goal is to help students learn to establish their own adaptive routines in multiple environments.

DEALING WITH SENSORY ISSUES

Most individuals with ASD experience significant discomfort around various sensory experiences (sensory defensiveness), or they may seek out particular sensory experiences (sensory seeking) for a number of reasons, including staying alert and/or feeling safe.

Early preparation

Children who present with hyper- or hypo-reactivity to sensory input will struggle in the classroom. If these issues are not addressed early on in the child's development, the child will struggle with learning and focusing. Sensory processing issues can involve sensitivity to stimuli in the following areas: auditory, visual, tactile, olfactory (smell), vestibular, and taste. In childhood, sensory integration therapy can help the child's nervous system gradually to tolerate more sensory input and protect the child from becoming easily overwhelmed. As students mature, they can learn to identify and implement various strategies to help themselves in the particular area of sensory processing that they struggle with. Collaboration with an occupational therapist will be essential for progress in this area.

Later preparation

In the college setting there will be all kinds sensory distractions and/or aversions, and students will have to identify and implement compensatory strategies so that these don't interfere in their focus and participation. Students who present with various sensory challenges should be learning ways to adapt in different environments throughout the course of their lives. There are many strategies for managing sensory disturbances, and a few of the more common ones that are popular with college students are outlined below.

- *Auditory* sensitivities can be managed at times by wearing lightweight earplugs in class, or listening to music through headphones in one's room. Students who need to wear earplugs will want to let the professor know, so that they can sit close enough to be able to hear the lecture. MP3 players are ideal for students who become overwhelmed when walking around a bustling college campus (Chew 2007) or when the noise level becomes distracting in the dorm (Coulter 2003). While some students find loud music disruptive, others may find it soothing. Some students are better able to focus on auditory information if they chew gum or suck on a lollipop.

- *Visual* sensitivities can be ameliorated by wearing colored lenses or sunglasses and using incandescent light. Fluorescent lighting can be extremely disruptive to someone with visual sensitivity—and unfortunately it seems that fluorescent lighting is the way of the future. Although light fixtures in dorms can be disabled and students can use their own incandescent lamps, this will not be possible in classrooms, so the student will need to find an appropriate way to accommodate. Some individuals experience visual disturbances, such as seeing lines that normally appear straight as curvy and/or broken. Wearing Irlen lenses may be useful for some students with visual sensitivities or visual distortions. Irlen lenses are colored lenses that are said to improve the manner in which the brain processes visual input (Irlen 1998). Students who are visually distracted will need to sit in a more remote area of the room, or in a cubicle. However, by the time students graduate from high school they should be able to manage a classroom environment without the need for a cubicle if they are to be successful in a college classroom.

- *Olfactory* sensitivity can be difficult because there are so many different smells everywhere one goes. Olfactory issues can be particularly bothersome in dormitories. It would not be unreasonable to ask to sit at a distance from a student who enjoys wearing perfume. It may also be possible to carry something with an appealing smell on it in order to reduce the intensity of other smells.

- Students with *tactile* sensitivities may enjoy wearing the same clothing over and over. They prefer soft fabrics, and strongly dislike tags in their clothing. Students need to learn that wearing the same clothing can have negative social consequences, especially if they don't launder those clothing items frequently enough to avoid having a distasteful odor.

- Finally, some students may simply become generally overwhelmed when many people are around. The conscious effort that goes into fitting in can also become overwhelming. Whatever the reason, students should know that taking breaks is acceptable. Some may find it useful to keep an array of objects around that they can use for calming and/or enhanced focus (e.g. thera-putty, small manipulatives, inflatable cushion on their seat, etc.). It will be important for the student with ASD to find a quiet place to relax or "decompress" while on campus (Chew 2007), because it won't always be feasible to go back to the dorm between classes. A Disabilities Services Advisor (DSA) can brainstorm with the student about possible solutions or compensatory strategies for sensory issues.

Strategies that facilitate the student's participation and focus should be included as an accommodation or modification to his educational programming throughout the elementary and high-school years. In an effort to foster greater self-awareness and independence, older students should be included in the process of selecting the types of accommodations or modifications that can help, and should also know why they need these strategies. The ultimate goal is to enable students to handle interfering sensory stimulation by learning how to tell when they're dysregulated and how to re-regulate themselves, and how to advocate for necessary accommodations independently.

Chapter 4

SELF-ADVOCACY SKILL SETS

The capacity to advocate for one's needs is the key to success for all of us. Standing up for ourselves, knowing what is good or bad for us, and understanding that it's not only possible but also important to make sure our needs are met, are essential for any of us to feel secure and happy. Students with autistic spectrum disorder (ASD) will need assistance and instruction for getting help when things aren't going as planned or expected. Self-advocacy is a complicated area. Some of the key factors involved are discussed below.

DISCLOSURE OF ONE'S DISABILITY

One of the main differences between high school and college is that high-school students with disabilities who attend public school (kindergarten to 12th grade) receive special education services through an Individualized Education Plan (IEP), or accommodations through a 504 Plan (a formal plan for the provision of specific, necessary accommodations to individuals with disabilities as specified by the Americans with Disabilities Act). (See Part III for discussion of the laws regulating secondary and post-secondary education practices.) Their disability is known to most adults who are involved in their education program. Students do have the right to decide whether or not to disclose having a disability to their peers in high school (if they even know they have one). Post-secondary education (PSE) institutions, on the other hand, are not subject to the education laws and protections afforded to younger students with disabilities by virtue of the Individuals with Disabilities Education Improvement Act (IDEA 2004). Therefore, colleges are not obligated to identify students with disabilities, or to provide them with an IEP or services of any kind. However, colleges in the United States that participate in federally funded student loans or receive any kind of federal monies are obligated to provide "reasonable accommodations" to individuals with medically documented disabilities, under Section 504 of the 1973 Rehabilitation Act and the Americans with Disabilities Act of 1990 (Johnson and Hines 2005). These colleges will have a Disabilities Services Office (DSO) available to students who are interested in receiving accommodations, but again, they are not obligated by law to identify students who need accommodations. In college, students are adults and are afforded the same decision-making powers that all adults in our society have in relation to themselves. What this means is that unless students voluntarily disclose that they have a disability, and provide the appropriate documentation, they will not receive accommodations. It is the student's choice. In making a decision to disclose one's disability in the PSE setting, the student should understand that self-disclosure can be done in a thoughtful manner with the main intent of enhancing the student's potential in that setting (Bliss and Edmonds 2008).

Early preparation

Young students should learn assertiveness and self-advocacy skills throughout their everyday lives. Students should be encouraged to talk to their teachers as early as possible whenever an issue arises, and, as much as possible, parents should avoid intervening once the student is able to fend for him- or herself. The more students learn to assert themselves, ask to have various needs met, speak up about things that bother them, etc., the better prepared they will be for the types of self-advocacy skills that they will need as young adults.

Later preparation

If students receive accommodations in high school that they find to be helpful, I strongly recommend that they plan on disclosing their disability and need for accommodations to the DSO on campus. With parental permission, I discuss issues of disclosure in my meetings with students, including an explanation of the student's disability, if that has not already taken place. Once students learn about their disability (see Chapter 1), education about disclosure incorporates criteria regarding who to disclose to, when it is appropriate/inappropriate to disclose, how to disclose, etc.

It's important to remember that the communication deficits inherent in ASD may make disclosure difficult for the student with ASD. Hesitancy to disclose should be explored to make sure that what looks like "resistance" is not the result of communication struggles. ASD is by nature a social communication disorder, and disclosure requires that individuals be able to communicate something very personal and important about themselves to another person. As a consequence of their disability, students with ASD (and possibly other students with language disabilities) would benefit from an accommodation that offers assistance (e.g. from an advisor or another designated person) in notifying professors of the student's disability and the types of accommodations the student needs. Some college advisors are willing to help students put together a comprehensive letter that they can hand to professors. With practice and experience most students will ultimately be able to handle this independently.

The decision about whether to disclose to roommates or other people on campus is up to the student. However, these decisions should be processed with the student *prior* to leaving home so that a plan can be made for how and to whom the student will disclose. There may be some very good reasons to educate classmates about ASD. Moore (2006) discusses the benefits one student reaped after her professor encouraged her to talk to her classmates about her cognitive challenges. According to Moore, the student's classmates "found a way to work with someone who opened up to them... Once she puts that on the table, what else can anyone feel embarrassed about having to divulge..." (p.5). While not all students will want or need to disclose to people other than professors and advisors, some students may want to consider meeting with the resident advisor (RA) in their dorm and with other students in nearby dorm rooms. (The RA is responsible for helping students adjust to dorm living, mediate between roommates when there are problems, and help make dorm living a fun experience.) The purpose of such a meeting would be to help others understand the student's behavior and know how to help and interact with the student.

Finally, I encourage students to introduce themselves to the campus Public Safety Office, so they can be made aware of any behaviors that might look suspicious, especially in times of duress. For example, one student who had epilepsy was having a type of seizure that made her appear violent. Public Safety was called, and because they didn't know about this student's seizure disorder, they assumed she was out of control and possibly on drugs. Their efforts to subdue her were unsuccessful (because she was in the throes of a seizure) so they handcuffed her and took her away in a Public Safety vehicle. Not only was it dangerous for the student to be handcuffed while having a seizure, she was humiliated and it took a great deal of convincing for Public Safety to realize that the student's behavior was related to her seizure disorder. Had they known and been educated about the student's medical condition in advance, they could have opted for a very different course of action.

UNDERSTANDING ONE'S LEARNING STYLE AND NEEDS, AND ASKING FOR THE APPROPRIATE ACCOMMODATIONS

All of us have particular learning styles. Some of us are auditory learners, some are visual learners. Some learn better when their bodies can be involved in the learning process (kinesthetic learners). These are characteristics that most typically developing students eventually learn about themselves—it's not uncommon when talking to high-school students to hear them say, "I learn best when I can take notes while listening," or "I'm an auditory learner and if I take notes I lose track of the lecture." (Some resources for assessing one's learning style are listed in Appendix B.)

Early preparation

Students with ASD may not learn these very important facts about themselves, and it will be important for their parents and educational team to involve them in the process of understanding how they learn and why certain strategies work for them. This process can begin as early as the third or fourth grade and is most effective when students are provided with real-life examples to highlight their particular learning styles. Specific facts and logical reasoning will help them understand why others describe their learning style in particular ways. In the early years examples will need to be more concrete, and will likely make more sense if they are shared with the student as they occur. When younger students are awarded accommodations, it's important for their teachers and support team members to educate them about why a particular accommodation is being implemented and how the accommodation is expected to help them. This may serve a double purpose. First and foremost, the student becomes educated about what helps her learn. Second, my hope would be that by being included in this process the student will subsequently be spared the sense that she is "cheating" by receiving accommodations. In this way students will develop a more open mind about asking for accommodations in college.

Later preparation

Students with ASD will need to understand aspects of their learning and rationales for accommodations throughout their elementary and high-school years. Currently, many of the high-school students I work with don't want accommodations. They don't understand why they need them, or why they receive them, and assume that their parents are working against them by trying to make things "easier" for them than for other students. This makes them feel "different." It creates tension between the students and their parents. Because parents are so involved in the students' programming, students feel as if they have no say in their education. They dream of the time when they will no longer be under their parents' rule and will finally get away from the things that have only served to make them feel different. My hope is that if students are included in decisions from early on, this process can be averted. Knowledge is power—students who know why they receive particular accommodations/interventions, and are included in evaluating whether or not these things work for them, will probably be more willing to carry this process into the college setting.

DEVELOPING MOTIVATION FOR NON-PREFERRED TOPICS

Those of us who work with individuals with ASD know that they have the capacity to attend to and engage in *preferred* tasks (i.e. tasks that they choose and enjoy) for hours on end, but struggle when required to participate in *non-preferred* tasks. In fact, this characteristic is seen so early in development that one of the most common initial goals written for very young children with ASD goes something like this: "Will engage in non-preferred tasks for increasingly longer periods of time." Time increments for this goal may start from as low as two minutes in three months' time, progressing to five minutes after six months, then seven minutes after nine months, because this behavior is so challenging to tackle. Young children who struggle in this area also have trouble with the most elementary aspects of learning—for example. paying attention even if you're not all that interested in the topic. According to Korpi (2008), "It is a combination of maturity, persistence, and a sense of responsibility that compels a person to keep on trying when faced with the less than enjoyable parts of a job. Acquiring persistence and a sense of responsibility are essential steps for the development of a work ethic" (p.27). Without this skill, students with ASD who later become workers with ASD will be unable to handle the multiple requirements of life in general.

Early preparation

The issue of preferred vs. non-preferred tasks is a big one and individuals with ASD can struggle with it throughout their lives. A young child who only likes to spin toys will resist becoming engaged in other tasks of less interest, even if his peers are playing around him. An older child who loves science will meticulously do science homework, but will struggle when it's time to do homework in less preferred subjects. This scenario raises the level of conflict in the family, leaving both parents and students feeling frustrated and helpless. Professionals must help parents find a way to address this issue systematically from the very beginning of the student's education.

It is important for individuals with ASD to understand themselves and to learn strategies that will help them find a balance between what they *have* to do, which usually falls into the non-preferred category, and what they *want* to do. We need to help younger students understand the draw to particular activities, while also understanding that non-preferred tasks are an important part of life. This type of awareness can be developed in younger children and teens in a number of different ways, including, but not limited to, the use of video modeling and Social Stories™ (Gray 1998). Preferred tasks can also be used as reinforcement for completion of non-preferred tasks. Students can learn to use a timer, so that they spend equal amounts of time completing homework in preferred and non-preferred subjects (e.g. one half-hour on each). Success can be rewarded with non-academic preferred tasks such as video games. Students may need to take breaks when engaging in non-preferred tasks, and they should be allowed to do so. The ultimate goal is to increase the amount of time the student can tolerate engaging in non-preferred tasks—academic or otherwise.

Later preparation

Students who have not developed the capacity to engage in non-preferred tasks by the late middle school to high school years struggle academically and socially. They are so skilled in resisting non-preferred tasks that they eventually get out of doing them—as a parent it simply becomes too difficult to battle with one's child over so many things. Particularly in this area, early programming and intervention are crucial. What is particularly challenging from a professional standpoint is that older students with this issue typically insist that if they really needed to do something, they would be able to. This is precisely the kind of thinking that can lead to failure in college because, in fact, they are often not able do what they think they can. When I have concerns that a student struggles in this area, I try to find a way to demonstrate that he or she needs help, although it can be difficult. I use real-life examples as provided by the student's parents. As we begin to understand more about why the student struggles with different tasks, one of the most common reasons is that he or she doesn't feel a particular task is important. Using Cognitive Behavioral Therapy (CBT) techniques to highlight inconsistencies in students' thought processes, older students may be able to reach an understanding of how these perceptions might interfere in their ability to succeed in college or in the workplace.

Many of my clients who begin taking college classes at local community colleges end up dropping, doing poorly in, or even failing their less preferred classes. I've worked with students who have been in community college settings for over five years as a result of this. Although I strongly believe that all students should be allowed to work at their own individual pace, this does not include putting off courses *ad infinitum* simply because they are not preferred, or are perhaps even too challenging. The goal of a college education is to help students develop skills and a knowledge base that will enable them to pursue employment, be as independent as possible, and become a contributing member of society. If a student is struggling to meet this goal, it's possible that he is not receiving an appropriate level of support in the college setting. It may also be possible that he has selected a course of study that is inappropriate for his abilities. Alternatively, his capacity to benefit from and complete a PSE also needs to be considered. This would be an appropriate juncture to consider obtaining a career/ vocational assessment to assist in determining the student's interests, strengths and weaknesses, and the best way to further his ability to develop his talents. Students who are struggling to complete coursework may benefit from taking a break from school, getting a job, embarking on an apprenticeship or internship, and returning to their studies after they've gained a bit of life experience and maturity. Unfortunately, many students resist this idea for a number of reasons. They may prefer to stay in a familiar setting, even though they're not meeting with success there. They may be frightened about getting a job or being in the "real world." They may feel like a failure if they "quit" school. Helping students understand and process their feelings about taking a break can help them make these important decisions with more clarity.

The issue of preferred vs. non-preferred tasks also arises in the marital work that I've done with couples where one person is believed to have ASD. Preferred tasks (often manifesting as "special interests") dominate the individual's focus and attention so much that other important things (e.g. the family's needs) fall by the wayside. With assistance the individual with ASD is able to see that the draw to the special interest is much stronger than the draw to engage, even with family members. Motivated individuals can work on this by setting up specific times for their special interest and specific times for family activities.

LEARN TO WORK IN A GROUP

It is no surprise that many students with ASD struggle with group projects. Group projects require the student to get along with and understand a number of people at the same time, and the social skills required for this task can be a challenge for many individuals with (and without) ASD. Often students may not understand the purpose of groupwork when they themselves can get things done faster on their own. Selection of group members can be problematic. If it is left to the students, the student with ASD may not be selected by others, or may not know how to identify appropriate peers. Groupwork requires the ability to be flexible about time, ideas and procedures. It also requires the ability to forgo one's own "brilliant" idea for another student's idea that may be more attractive to the entire group than to the student with ASD. Finally, groupwork can be very challenging for individuals with rigid thinking.

Early preparation

Families of younger children can practice the basics of being in a group: taking turns selecting and doing activities, picking restaurants, sitting in different places at the dinner table, etc. These activities also occur in the school setting. Calendars that identify whose turn it is for that day will make this process more palatable for the child with ASD. Flexibility is key here. One child insisted on always being the one to lock the car doors with the remote, and since the child didn't have any siblings, his parents allowed this behavior. I saw this as an excellent opportunity to build in turn-taking and flexibility, so I suggested that the parents take turns using the remote with the child. Parents should be alert to whenever the child insists on doing a particular activity or behavior all the time, and use this as an opportunity to build in flexibility.

Developmentally, children learn to work in dyads before they're able to work in small, and then larger, groups. Play dates would be considered dyadic, and many students with ASD struggle on play dates because they only want to do what interests them. I encourage parents to use the 'Activity choice chart' on p.103 to help children develop the turn-taking capacity necessary for play dates and ultimately for working in groups. During a play date, each child selects four or five preferred activities. Then they take turns engaging in one another's activities for a specified length of time, which is monitored with a mechanical timer. In this way both children know that the time is fair, there is no negotiating for more time unless both children are in agreement, and the timer signals the transition to the other child's chosen activity. Group skills can be developed by playing cooperative games where the child works with others on a team to reach a mutual goal. Team members strategize about the best methods to reach their goal and work together towards that end. Children can practice these skills one-to-one with adults (e.g. family members and other professionals) who can help the child learn teamwork skills. Following skill development, practice begins with other children. It may be necessary for a professionally trained adult to facilitate for some time, as this will likely be very challenging for the child. However, the results will be incredibly valuable in the child's future.

Later preparation

Although students may struggle a great deal in this area, I do not recommend awarding an accommodation that permits a student to work alone, especially at the outset. While there are some careers that may not require a great capacity to work in a group, "no man is an island" and for the most part the nature of human society makes it essential to be able to function within some kind of group setting at least some of the time. Therefore, intervention and training should continue into the high-school years in as many settings as possible. Many individuals report that as adults they are better able to tolerate some activities that they simply could not tolerate as children. Therefore, just because a student was unable to work in a group in high school, that doesn't mean that the student won't be able to do so in college, although facilitation and coaching by a peer or other type of mentor may be necessary at first. Developing the ability to work in a group will help the student meet with greater success not only in college, but also in the workplace and in any future family or other communal settings.

Some of the challenges of working in groups that students experience in the college setting are discussed in the existing literature. According to Perner (2007), "…the more brainy person may get stuck with a disproportionate amount of work" due to varying levels of motivation in group members. He notes that scheduling groupwork sessions can be challenging for the individual with ASD, especially when procrastination results in stress and having to make last-minute decisions. Group sessions can be stressful when the group needs to meet outside of class because it interferes with the student's routine and need for sameness. Harpur *et al.* (2004) note that students may not be able to schedule group projects around their own routines and will have to take into consideration the responsibilities and availability of others in the group. They also suggest that students use their "analytical abilities to identify a component of the project that is suited to their talents and state of knowledge of the course at that point in time" (p.63) in an effort to avoid being assigned something that is not geared to the student's liking or level of interest. This is one way for students to advocate for themselves within the context of a group of peers. Finally, Palmer (2006) suggests keeping a list of the other students in the group, including their phone numbers and email addresses, and notating group meetings in one's calendar. Social and communication skills are at the heart of being able to work in a group, and these skills constitute the primary challenges faced by individuals with ASD. Coaching and other accommodations may be necessary in the college setting.

LEARN ABOUT THE GRADING SYSTEM AND KEEP TRACK OF GRADES

Most typically developing students take an interest in the grading system of each individual instructor, and most students have a reasonable idea of what their grades are in each of their classes at any given time. In my experience, many students with ASD find grading systems complicated and daunting. Each teacher uses a slightly (or distinctly) different system, the concept of grading curves and point systems can be confusing, and grades are often perceived as subjective or arbitrary (Solove 2006). Grading systems have a distinct social component, in that they inherently compare students to one another. This adds a layer of confusion for the student with ASD. When grades are posted, students can feel confused about why one person's grade is better or worse than their own. All of these factors may be difficult for students with ASD to understand, resulting in what can appear to be indifference about their grades.

Early preparation

If we understand the challenges inherent in deciphering grading systems, then we can take measures to help reduce confusion and anxiety by specifically educating students about the grading system throughout their schooling, beginning as soon as grades make a difference. Once students understand their grades, programs can be developed to heighten their interest in and motivation about their own grades. However, in doing so we must be careful not to trigger a student's perfectionistic strivings to get all "A"s.

One strategy that can heighten students' interest in their grades is to present the grading system as a way for them to establish goals for themselves—a way to beat one's personal best or compete against oneself. For example, the student can strive for a realistic grade in each class (some classes are easier or harder than others), and in order to keep up with her progress she has to keep track of her grades on individual assignments and tests, perhaps by recording them in a special notebook. Once again, this needs to be programmed into the student's educational plan because, as with many other skills, students with ASD may not instinctively pick up on what they need to do to improve their grades. This confusion may manifest as a student's lack of interest in her grades. Teachers play a big role in this process. They need to be enlisted to meet with students on a regular basis, explain specifically why students received particular grades on an assignment, and let them know what they need to do to improve their grades on subsequent assignments.

Later preparation

Specificity in grading assignments can make a big difference in high school. For example, some teachers may place a red check mark next to a paragraph without indicating why. This can be extremely confusing to the student. The fact that the check mark is red could mean something negative, or the fact that the paragraph has a check mark at all could mean that it's well written. After years of this type of confusion, students who may not be able to verbalize their confusion may simply lose interest in their grades. Teachers need to check for understanding of assignment and test instructions, as many students with ASD will think they understand the instructions when in actuality they do not. If they think they understand, they will not ask for clarification, so checking for understanding needs to be part of the student's educational plan from the start. The more specific information students receive about what is expected on each individual assignment and what they will be graded on, the more likely it is that they will be engaged in meeting their personal goals. Because generalization is a common problem for students with ASD, care should be taken to ensure that students understand grading systems and expectations in the college setting. One of the most effective strategies to clarify grades and expectations is to make them visual. The use of an "if…then…" or other type of flow chart can be used to help students understand expectations and how their performance will be evaluated.

Chapter 5

ORGANIZATIONAL SKILL SETS

Organizational skills do not come naturally to all of us. Students with ASD in particular may struggle more than other students in this area and will benefit from specific instruction and skill development, starting as early as possible. Because organization may not come naturally and will probably not be enjoyable, many students will avoid doing it or keeping up with it. The skills discussed in this chapter need to be learned prior to leaving home for college, so as to reduce what I deem to be unnecessary stress. I say "unnecessary" because some of these skills can be relatively easy to learn and incorporate into one's life if they are programmed in from the start. Stress as a result of lack of basic proficiency in this and other areas can only serve to increase the student's already fragile sense of security. In spite of the inherent challenges in acquiring organizational skills, development in this area will lead to greater independence overall.

As students mature, they need to be included in the process of organizing their own backpacks, putting assignments into their respective places immediately after completing them, learning systems for keeping track of their personal belongings, and learning how to manage their time in order to plan ahead for tests and other more lengthy projects. While it may be a struggle, it is very important for parents not to do these things for their child. If a student is struggling with organization in the areas listed above, parents can ask teachers or other professionals on his intervention team for assistance. Behavioral strategies and the use of visual calendars, whiteboards, Post-It™ notes, or any other "prop" that works for a particular student, can be instrumental in facilitating greater organizational skills. Poor organizational skills in the college setting can be devastating for obvious reasons, and can also lead to crippling levels of anxiety.

ORGANIZING PERSONAL DOCUMENTS AND BELONGINGS

There are many ways to incorporate organization tasks into the young child's life at home and at school. Requiring older children to be responsible for their own belongings and their schoolwork will enable them to meet with greater success in their secondary and post-secondary education.

Early preparation

Even young students can learn various types of organization systems for their personal belongings and school assignments. They can learn to keep an address book for their friends and family members, how to address envelopes, have a file in which to keep all of their awards, etc. Early organizational skills also involve learning to put toys and other personal belongings away in the appropriate place. Using visual cues (e.g. matching colors or pictures and later, words) can in due course be translated into developing systems for organizing school assignments. I've worked with many families who, in the interest of ensuring that their child succeeds, become unwittingly over-involved in making sure their child turns in perfectly completed homework. Parents may also find the struggle of helping a resistant child organize his backpack overwhelming and time-consuming. Understandably, they often take over that function. Professionals and parents need to find a balance between helping the child and dis-empowering the child by doing things for him that he can do himself (Iland 2008). We also want to avoid developing an unhealthy dependency that may be difficult to break later on. To this end, it may be useful for the child to be accountable to a professional, rather than to his parents, when working in this area. It may also be helpful to have the assistance of a therapist or other type of interventionist who comes to the home to design and implement behavioral programs and organizational tools to help increase the child's organizational skills.

Later preparation

Organization of one's personal documents becomes more sophisticated as one matures. Older students should participate with a parent to learn how to maintain their medical files and understand medical and auto insurance. Medical conditions, medications and contacts can be carried in a wallet in case of emergency. Financial organization goes along with organizing one's personal documents, but will be discussed below under money management. Any systems that were in place for younger students should be expanded on as students mature. All of the systems mentioned in the introductory paragraph to this section should be maintained by the student with decreasing adult supervision.

Students who go away for college need a central location such as a notebook or file box that contains pertinent medical information, insurance forms (if needed), important addresses and phone numbers, pre-printed address labels for family members, bank records and a way of storing statements, and birthday listings for family members (Coulter 2003). It is also a good idea to have students pre-program their phones with important telephone numbers, including family, friends, and any important on-campus numbers. Inputting important email addresses into their computer before leaving home will also be very useful.

USING A PLANNER FOR MAKING, RECORDING, KEEPING, BEING ON TIME FOR, AND CANCELING APPOINTMENTS

Learning that one is responsible to others and that one must respect others' time by honoring their appointments or canceling appropriately is an important social skill for older teens and young adults. Developing independence and good follow-through will ensure that students demonstrate responsibility to others.

Early preparation

Basic calendar skills are at the core of the ability to understand and successfully utilize a planner, and can be learned very early on. Parents and teachers of students with ASD should incorporate calendar use and independent follow-through into the students' overall programming so that these skills carry over into high school.

Later preparation

Learning to use a planner to record assignments, due dates, etc., is essential for success in college and beyond. Most adults use a variety of different strategies (e.g. organizers, electronic calendars, notes) to keep track of appointments, projects, etc. While most of us didn't need specific instruction in how to use these tools, students with ASD will need instruction and ongoing guidance. Because it's such an important skill, it needs to be programmed into a student's Individualized Education Plan (IEP) at the middle and high school levels. Students who do not have an IEP at school may need to work with an educational therapist.

What will probably not be mastered in high school is the skill of remembering appointments, because parents are usually at the helm of the student's schedule and most high-school students are not required to make or cancel their own appointments. However, parents can include their child in this process as much as possible, fostering greater independence as the child matures. Students can learn to use their planners to keep track of appointments with school counselors, advisors, and teachers, and can also be held accountable for keeping, canceling or rescheduling those appointments as appropriate. Parents can reinforce this process by keeping a visual schedule of the family's activities, appointments, etc., in the home. Finally, older high-school students can begin to participate in scheduling and canceling their own medical appointments.

College students are expected to be completely independent in completing and turning in their assignments, making it impossible for any student to succeed in college without some type of system to help them coordinate their studies and remember when to turn things in. There are ample reasons to make appointments in the college setting, including appointments with professors, advisors, other students, support staff (e.g. tutors), and possibly doctors and therapists. If students cannot perform this function, they will be at a great disadvantage. Keep in mind that although a student may have learned to use a planner in high school, she may need support in transferring this skill into the college setting. Students who struggle in this area may find it helpful to work with a time management tutor.

RESPONDING TO EMAIL

Although many individuals with ASD prefer online communication over most other more interactive forms of communication (e.g. telephone or in-person), there are some students who are not interested in emailing or using communication methods such as text or instant messaging. These students will need to receive specific instruction in email use, as emailing is a commonly used method of communication between students and professors.

Early preparation

Although younger students typically don't use email, they can learn the prerequisite reciprocity skills that this involves. These include basic conversation skills, understanding that communication is a back and forth process—when someone asks a question they expect a response. By the time many students enter middle school they use cell phones, and text messaging is a very popular way for teenagers to communicate with one another. Some parents are against giving their child a cell phone at such a young age, and although I respect each parent's right to make these types of decisions, I also encourage them to consider the benefits of affording their child with ASD the opportunity to participate in these important social activities. Most parents have been willing to consider a cell phone as long as the child understands safety factors, limits for use, and the consequences of transgressions.

Later preparation

Once students are mature enough to use email, they need to understand the basic principles of emailing: that the sender of an email expects some type of response from the recipient. Although this may seem obvious to most of us, some of the students I've worked with do not automatically respond to emails, and this has gotten them into trouble. For example, a student who received an email from her professor took note of the information in the email, and did not feel the need to respond. As a result, the professor didn't know whether the student had received the email and felt annoyed when she didn't respond, which was then confusing to the student. This is a classic example of how something that seems so basic and obvious to most of us is not always experienced that way by individuals with ASD. Unfortunately, when these types of things happen, students can be seen as being defiant or having an "attitude." Students need to be taught that when they receive an email, the appropriate response is to reply to the email, even if only to say that they have received and understood the content of the email. I've approached this issue by explaining to students that an email or text message is like a conversation, so that when someone sends them something it means that he or she has started the conversation and is waiting for a response. I practice this with students by sending them emails and letting them know I expect some type of response from them. This is something that can easily be incorporated into a student's programming both at home and in school. Parents, siblings, other family members, and teachers can communicate with students using various electronic modes with the understanding that the student is expected to respond. This type of practice will be invaluable to students in the college setting.

Social networking on the internet is also a common form of communication. Students need to know and agree to abide by specific safety guidelines. Although it may be difficult to monitor all of the student's communications, there have been many instances of inappropriate content being used by students who did not understand that other people might be offended or concerned. I encourage parents to use as many safeguards as possible on their home computer systems and to educate themselves on how to protect their child's safety in this medium.

KNOW HOW TO BREAK DOWN, ORGANIZE, AND SEQUENCE HOMEWORK ASSIGNMENTS, HOW TO BREAK DOWN COURSE MATERIAL INTO MANAGEABLE CHUNKS, AND OTHER TASKS RELATED TO THE EXECUTIVE FUNCTIONS OF THE BRAIN

This is one of the most challenging areas for individuals with ASD, as well as those with other types of learning disabilities/differences. Skills in this and other areas fall into what are known as "executive functions" (EF). EF are brain-based activities that enable us to "see the big picture"; make decisions based on our own awareness of the potential outcomes of our behavior or choices; organize material, as well as estimate the time frame allotted for a particular task, and plan accordingly; and make modifications based on new information (Attwood 2007). EF deficits affect the individual's perceptions, the manner in which one sequences the steps necessary to complete tasks, the way material is organized and prioritized in the brain, and the ability to direct one's focus and attention appropriately (Perry 2009). In attempting to understand the relationship between executive function deficits and behavioral difficulties common in ASD, Gilotty *et al.* (2002) note that it is possible to predict deficits in all areas of adaptive functioning in individuals with ASD who exhibit lowered abilities in the EF skills of "initiate" and "working memory" (see pp.95–96, 99), "suggesting that impairments in executive abilities are strongly associated with the deficits in communication, play and social relationships found in children with autism" (p.241).

At this point in time, most school systems do not formally assess EF deficits in students. They rely primarily on tests of intelligence and academic ability to identify learning challenges. Even when students are privately assessed as having EF deficits, most school systems do not offer formal instruction in this area. Delis *et al.* (2007) note that "IQ and EF skills are relatively divergent cognitive domains and…IQ tests do not provide a sufficient or comprehensive assessment of higher-level executive functions" (p.37). The findings of their study suggest that some school-age children are better at "rote-verbal skills" than abstract thinking. These children may experience academic success but not receive intervention in areas of weakness because school systems typically de-emphasize the latter and place emphasis on the former. Many students with ASD fall into this category. Alternatively, the study indentifies another group of students, who exhibit weaknesses in rote-verbal skills and strengths in "higher-level executive functions such as abstract thinking, cognitive flexibility, and problem-solving skills" (p.38). Students in this group typically do more poorly on instruments assessing IQ and achievement, and on college entrance exams, and "these tests may represent roadblocks to areas of study that could benefit from the creativity that these students offer" (p.38). As such, the authors suggest that "school and university systems…strive to broaden the scope of their cognitive evaluations to include tests of both rote knowledge and higher-level executive functions" (p.39). By determining each student's relative strengths and weaknesses we will be better equipped to guide students into careers for which they are best suited.

In light of the potentially devastating sequelae of executive dysfunction, all individuals with ASD should be evaluated early in their educational careers to determine which of these brain functions need attention and remediation. Ongoing re-evaluation will be important to address more sophisticated, higher level functions. Individuals with EF deficits must be involved in remediation as early as possible, and will benefit from working with an educational therapist as well as a psychologist with expertise in ASD. These professionals can help students and families learn different ways to structure the home environment to foster optimum development in this area.

Remember that EFs are intertwined and inter-related, meaning that it is usually impossible to have impairment in just one area, although individuals with EF deficits do exhibit strengths as well as weaknesses. The goal of treatment would be to use the individual's strengths to develop compensatory strategies for weaker abilities. I often work closely with educational and speech and language therapists who are highly skilled at helping students to develop these skills.

After reading the material below, you will see that the characteristics commonly attributed to some individuals with ASD (lazy, unmotivated, bored, avoidant, oppositional, distracted, etc.) actually do them an injustice. Placing these labels onto a student is harmful in many ways and misses the point entirely, which is to find ways to help students when they struggle. These labels send negative messages, which will undermine the student's self-esteem for years. They also engender the feeling of being misunderstood, which results in further isolation. Students who are struggling should be evaluated by a neuropsychologist so that the true origins of their challenges can be identified and remediated. This type of evaluation can also be used to obtain accommodations in college and in the workplace (see Chapter 10). Once EF deficits are identified, then true assistance can be provided to help the student maximize abilities and develop compensatory skills for specific deficits. Once again, the earlier these issues can be identified, the longer the student receives remediation for them, the better off that student will be in a college setting.

While researchers and others who study and write about EF may agree on the most commonly identified EFs, there is also variability amongst them. Several of the most common EFs will be described below. However, I will not spend a great deal of time providing suggestions for early and later preparation as above, due to the incredibly complex and varied nature of these brain functions.

Initiation

This skill involves the ability to independently and efficiently initiate a task with minimal procrastination (Dawson and Guare 2004). Students who function efficiently in this area are able to pursue and sustain focus on a task in spite of distractions. Some authors also suggest that the ability to generate ideas, answers, and solutions are also aspects of initiation (Gioia et al. 2000). Individuals who struggle with initiation often want to succeed but just can't find a way to get started with a task, and they need excessive prompting. This need for excessive prompting and guidance can result in individuals with EF deficits being exploited (Perry 2009). According to Perry, there are five elements to initiation:

- alertness
- awareness of options
- response to internal and external cues
- evaluation of choices for appropriateness
- action.

It's important to remember that EF skills and deficits are complicated and can affect an individual in multiple areas. For example, in some individuals poor organizational skills may be the cause of their difficulty in getting started on a task.

While students who struggle in this area can appear oppositional, a true EF deficit is not a compliance issue. However, compliance issues and/or oppositional behavior in some individuals may not have anything to do with an EF deficit. These individuals may have the capacity to initiate, but do not wish to comply. A thorough evaluation will be needed to determine the root causes of these behaviors.

Planning and organizing

Planning enables us to imagine and develop goals for ourselves or for our projects and then determine the appropriate steps needed to accomplish those goals. The ability to do this assumes that one is able to anticipate future events, to sequence and put together a number of steps in a timely manner, and that one can independently follow directions with multiple steps (Gioia *et al.* 2000; Richard and Fahy 2005). Organizing involves the ability to develop a system to keep track of our work and express ourselves in a well-organized manner, be it in writing or orally. Incorporated in organizing is the ability to tease out and understand multiple and main topics in written, auditory or visual material (e.g. books, lectures or movies). Visual organization enables one to scan a complicated array of visual material in order to make meaning out of it.

Individuals who struggle in this area often have trouble expressing their ideas in writing, in spite of having good ideas. They appear overwhelmed by large amounts of information and frequently get caught up in details. They may frequently appear to "miss the forest for the trees" or, as one adult with Asperger's noted, "Not only did I not see the forest for the trees; I was so intensely distracted that I missed the trees for the species of lichen on their bark" (Page 2007).

Organizing also extends to individuals' ability to keep their personal space and belongings in an orderly manner so that they can find the things they need in order to do their work. Often individuals who struggle in this area have chaotic and messy desks, rooms, and backpacks (Dawson and Guare 2004; Gioia *et al.* 2000). What's important to remember is that "It's not that the person doesn't organize his world, it's that the person's brain isn't organized" (Perry 2009, p.69), and so they don't realize that they have to think about the various steps needed to complete a particular task. Helping students learn to verbalize and even write out the steps they will need to take before beginning a task can help with planning and organization. Planning can also be developed by completing simple activities such as mazes, or identifying the steps to make a bowl of cereal or do a book report, etc. Breaking tasks down into discrete steps by diagramming can also help individuals visually distinguish and organize a task.

Perry (2009) suggests that individuals be given assignments one step at a time in order to mitigate the consequences of poor planning and organizing in the workplace. In the college setting students can learn to break assignments into manageable chunks before actually beginning the assignment. Whether in the workplace or school setting, reminders or visual charts should be used for tasks with multiple steps. Perry notes that an inability to plan one's life across time can make people who have this deficit appear "ageless" because "they don't seem to register the passage of time or changes in social conventions…they continue to talk of things they will do 'in the future' long after the time has passed for those events to be pursued or given up" (pp.70–71). I've worked with many clients who continue their studies at a junior college well into their twenties, with full intent to begin a four-year university course afterwards. They cannot imagine the impact and implications of being a 25+ year-old undergraduate student. Deficits in social awareness interfere in their ability to understand that employers might think twice about hiring a 30-year-old person who just completed their undergraduate studies. Finally, they don't seem to have a sense of how they plan to become self-sufficient and live independently.

Clearly, the impact of a deficit in planning and organization is far-reaching and may have negative implications for the individual's ability to make decisions, understand the passage of time, develop and carry out daily routines, and more.

Self-monitoring

Self-monitoring is an aspect of metacognition, the ability to observe oneself in various situations. It also involves the ability to check our work or tests for mistakes, proofread our papers and, in general, take the necessary time to produce a good product. Monitoring also reaches into our interactions with others, in noticing and identifying the effect our behavior has on others, and using the information to modify our behavior (Dawson and Guare 2004; Gioia *et al.* 2000; Richard and Fahy 2005). There are many reasons why some people are better at this than others, but most individuals with ASD struggle in this area. As a result, their interpersonal responses (or lack thereof) may often be judged as being self-involved, uncaring, or unsympathetic. For example, individuals with ASD are notorious for expressing themselves without censorship, which can often lead to hurt feelings. Their penchant for telling the truth often leads them astray in their social encounters. While people with ASD may afterwards be able to see that their statements could have been hurtful, monitoring deficits render them unable to make this judgment and modify their behavior in the moment.

Perry (2009) notes that self-monitoring deficits interfere in all aspects of an individual's social life. The individual "may be lax in their hygiene, or dress eccentrically; their conversation is self-focused, or they make their desires known without regard for the social cues of the other" (p.102). When their interactions fail as a result of these and other characteristics, they struggle to understand what possible role their behavior or decisions might have had or why others do not care to spend time with them. As mentioned above, although their monitoring difficulties can make them appear as if they don't care, the last thing on their minds is consciously to hurt or offend anyone. However, their inability to monitor their choices, behaviors, thought processes, and so on, derails the typical development of self-reflection and deprives them of the opportunity to learn from their experiences (Perry 2009). Monitoring has a great deal to do with self-awareness and awareness of others, so if an individual has impairments in this area it will only make these tasks more challenging.

An excellent strategy to enhance self-monitoring skills is to have students learn to monitor and record their own behaviors for short periods of time or during specific times of the day. Students who struggle with this can view videotapes of themselves and others while learning to identify and record behavior. After recording their own behavior, they can learn to evaluate it (e.g. on- or off-task; preferred or non-preferred, etc.). This strategy can also be taken on in more structured social situations (e.g. social skills facilitation groups) by videotaping students interacting with one another and later viewing the tapes to learn how to identify specific positive or negative social behaviors. The goal of these activities is for students to develop the ability to consciously monitor themselves and to improve their overall behavior in multiple environments.

Working memory

A highly researched area of executive dysfunction, working memory is commonly identified as an area of challenge in many individuals with ASD. Some researchers suggest that working memory impairments can be used to distinguish between individuals with ASD and individuals with learning disabilities (Barnard *et al.* 2008). Working memory enables us to complete tasks by hanging onto necessary information in our minds. Strong skills in this area help us follow complex and multi-step directions and activities, and complete mental arithmetic. Often individuals with poor working memory cannot remember things even for a few seconds. If sent on an errand, they may forget what it was they were supposed to be doing. When working on a task, they may forget what they're doing midstream. They may also struggle to apply previous experiences or learning to the current situation (Dawson and Guare 2004). At times they may lose track of the rules even as they're involved in a task. Mental manipulation tasks are very difficult (Gioia *et al.* 2000) and they may need to write things down in order to remember and solve orally presented problems. It may be difficult to stick with or maintain attention and focus during a task, and often the individual will switch to another task midstream and fail to complete the one that he abandoned. Paraphrasing reading passages can help with working memory while reading, as can simple tasks that challenge a student to listen to details or instructions and then carry them out at a later time. Individuals who struggle with working memory benefit greatly from using planners, visual cues/reminders, and self-talk during tasks to ensure they've covered the steps necessary for completion.

Shift/flexibility

The ability to shift our attention and interest enables us to make transitions, be flexible, and alternate our attention between one task and another. Multi-tasking requires a great deal of shifting, monitoring, and making judgments and changes about what we are doing while we are doing it. Individuals who have severe deficits in this area often appear to "get stuck" and exhibit repetitive or perseverative behavior. They can be rigid and inflexible and need very consistent routines in their lives. It is difficult for them to let go of their own topics of interest in conversations, and in private they pursue those interests fervently. Disappointments can become fixations and it can be difficult to move on from them. Changes in routine are met with repetitive questioning about when an upcoming activity will take place. Problem-solving is usually a challenge and can be affected by rigidity and/or by repeated implementation of the same solution, even if it doesn't work (Gioia *et al.* 2000; Perry 2009).

Activities designed to help students learn to do things differently from how they've done them in the past are beneficial in developing shift and flexibility. While routines are extremely important in some aspects of life, students also need to learn to tolerate uncertainty and to adapt to changes in their environments. Exposing them to novel circumstances with positive outcomes will foster greater tolerance of change. Encouraging students to brainstorm about vague situations or re-design a previously designed structure will foster both flexibility and creativity. Finally, having students rank different things such as likes and dislikes from "most to least desirable" or ranges of emotions from "subtle to less subtle" will help them be less "absolute" or black-and-white in the way they perceive the world.

Response inhibition

Response inhibition enables us to control our impulses and stop our behavior when appropriate. It encompasses all of the skills inherent in the expression, "think before you act" (Dawson and Guare 2004). Individuals with poor inhibition can be perceived as intrusive, often interrupting or disrupting ongoing activities. They also have trouble understanding personal space and have a poor sense of safety. They have a high level of energy and can at times exhibit physical responses that are inappropriate for the situation. Inhibition is also related to emotional regulation/self-regulation, and so individuals may appear to have no control over their emotional reactions and/or behavior. They exhibit inappropriate modulation of their emotions and do not always take into consideration the environment and the expectations of other people. Individuals with ASD may have fewer coping strategies to regulate high levels of anxiety or intense bouts of anger. Facilitating the development of multiple, useful strategies for self-regulation can, with a great deal of practice, go a long way towards helping students learn to inhibit their emotional reactions appropriately. Activities that require the student to stop doing or responding to something, or to wait, can help develop this skill. Relaxation strategies can also be used, but must be practiced regularly.

DEVELOP TECHNIQUES TO GRASP THE "BIG PICTURE" CONCEPTS

A related group of brain functions or information processing skills that have also been highly researched are incorporated into what is called *central coherence* (CC): the ability to integrate information into a larger context. Deficits in CC appear as an inability to extract higher-level meaning (Frith 1989; Frith and Happe 1994). There is a great deal of controversy in the research literature about the role of CC in ASD, but many individuals with ASD are reported to have weak CC. While individuals with ASD have a strong capacity to focus intently on detail, they can also miss the broader context (Attwood 2007). Students with challenges in this area often have trouble comprehending more sophisticated reading material, understanding the interwoven plots of movies or plays, and also following multiple conversations and classroom discussions. It can also be difficult for them to understand what information is most important in texts, conversations or lectures.

Early preparation

Early assessment of a student's abilities in this area with concomitant *ongoing* intervention is crucial. I stress the ongoing nature of intervention because, while it is very common for students to receive intervention until they have "mastered" the skills needed for their current developmental level, most will also need intervention for skills required at higher levels of development. Intervention includes learning effective study skills, how to identify the salient aspects of the material being learned, and strategies for taking notes and making note cards.

Later preparation

As students mature, they will likely require ongoing intervention in this area due to the increasingly sophisticated nature of the material that they have to learn. This applies not only to written information, but also to auditory information, including lectures and conversations. Some parents are surprised when I recommend speech and language therapy for their teenager. After all, why send someone who is fluently verbal for speech and language therapy? Just as written material becomes more sophisticated over time, lectures and conversations also become more sophisticated, and the student with ASD will likely not keep up with the complex rules of communication. An example of this is sarcasm, which is often incorporated into college lectures.

Therapists play a key role in educating other professionals, parents, and students about the complex, evolving nature of skill development in all areas, so that when further therapies are recommended no time is lost in obtaining them.

CREATE ROUTINES TO HELP MANAGE STUDY/LEISURE TIME, AND DEVELOP THE ABILITY TO TOLERATE NON-PREFERRED TASKS

The students that I work with experience significant challenges in this area due to difficulties with information processing and executive functioning. Students struggle with time management, and often prefer to spend most of their time on their particular preferred activities (video games, computer, internet, comic books, etc.). Parents continually complain about having to fight with students about doing homework, and often the student needs to be monitored for any number of reasons. Learning to structure one's time is essential for managing one's life, especially in college where the familiar structure of home is, for all practical purposes, gone. A challenge in this area lies in balancing the need to establish routines with the concomitant need to develop flexibility.

Early preparation

Skill development in this area must begin from as early in the child's life as possible. I will detail strategies in this section rather than in the

"Later preparation" section that follows, but it is important that these strategies are practiced throughout the individual's development.

There are a number of techniques that can be used. Overall, I encourage families of young children to begin implementing the concept of daily routines at home as a part of the family culture. In this way students learn, from as far back as they can remember, that routines are important and valued. As they mature, new routines can be added.

If we look closely at the lives of young students, their schedules are almost always managed by the adults around them. In order for young students with ASD to understand the concept of scheduling, they should be involved in the process of determining their own personal schedules. The TEACCH approach (Treatment and Education of Autistic and related Communication-handicapped CHildren; see Appendix B) from the University of North Carolina does this by allowing students to structure the order in which they complete their academic work in the classroom. Students who have a say in how they organize their time tend to stick to that schedule with fewer prompts and more consistency. Therefore, whenever the environment is flexible enough for the student to have a say, she should take part in designing her own schedule. In the home setting students can be a part of the process of determining how they go about their morning and other daily routines, or their after-school homework schedules. While I am not advocating allowing students to dictate how they manage their time, they need to be included in the process. This includes negotiating with parents about how much or little time is spent on any given activity. Posting up the schedules also serves as an aid to developing greater independence in managing one's time. Finally, the use of a timer minimizes the amount of "nagging" parents have to do, and facilitates greater independence and a sense of mastery in students.

Even preschoolers can participate in creating schedules with their parents and in school. Older students will have a say in the actual schedule, how the schedule looks (so that it makes sense to them), and where the schedule is posted, while younger students will enjoy helping parents make and decorate their schedules. Visual charts can also be helpful with play dates, which can be difficult for children with ASD when they have to engage in non-preferred activities. Therefore, I recommend that parents make an activity choice chart consisting of two columns, one for the child and one for the playmate. This can be done by using a sheet of paper or a whiteboard. Each child selects three to four activities, and they take turns engaging in each of their choices for a specified length of time throughout the play date, using a timer.

This model can also be used to help children who struggle when asked to engage in non-preferred tasks. A leisure time choice chart can be made by using a piece of board (e.g. cardboard, whiteboard) that has several Velcro™ dots on it. Because this is a leisure chart, I recommend that the Velcro™ dots be placed randomly on the cardboard. Small cards with activity choices in written and/or picture format are attached to the

ACTIVITY CHOICE CHART

	ME	MY FRIEND
Crafts		
Board Games		
Reading		
Play Outside		
Watch TV		
Play with Pets		
Computer Games		
Homework		
Cooking		
Listen to Music		
Play Video Games		
Art (color, painting...)		
Make Believe Play		
Dress Up		
Clean Room		
Call a Friend		
Build Stuff (legos, blocks...)		
Laundry		

dots. Before beginning an activity the child selects the corresponding card from the chart. Once the activity has been completed (either by the child or as signaled by a timer), the card is stored in an envelope or small plastic bag.

Choices should always include preferred and non-preferred activities, and if necessary, the child can be required to alternate between them. Also, both preferred and non-preferred activities should appear multiple times on a chart so that the child sees that there are multiple opportunities to engage in a preferred activity. In this way the leisure time choice chart also becomes useful as a tool for developing time management skills. The child learns that after engaging in a non-preferred activity (e.g. homework), he can select a more desirable activity (e.g. computer). Activity choices can be time-limited (by using a timer), which limits the amount of time the child engages in both preferred and non-preferred tasks, and takes the onus off the parent to be in "control" of the time. The goal of the leisure time choice chart is to instill the notion that sometimes in life we have to do things we don't necessarily want to do, but we also get opportunities to do the things we like to do. Examples of activities that can be posted on this chart will vary, based on each individual child, but some that have been used by my own clients include: computer time, video games, crafts, drawing, going outside, television, reading, board games, walking the dog, helping mom cook, homework, practicing one's instrument, etc.

The professional's role in this process is very important. In addition to helping the family determine when a visual schedule would be helpful and how to develop the schedule, older students can be accountable to the professional rather than to the parents. While students may initially need prompting to use their schedules, the goal is to develop independence in doing so. During follow-up meetings with the student and the family we discuss the student's adherence to the schedule, or lack thereof, and develop strategies to facilitate greater cooperation. It may be necessary to develop a behavioral program to increase the student's participation. However, there are numerous inherent rewards for complying with this task. First and foremost, family tension and conflict is significantly reduced because parents no longer have to "nag" the student to complete necessary tasks. Second, students develop a sense of pride and feel industrious when they independently move from activity to activity. Finally, students learn an important skill that can transfer to other situations, albeit with guidance at first.

Later preparation

Teenagers and young adults with ASD need to make conscious choices about how to approach the various tasks in their lives. This process is made easier when they have learned how to determine the frequency and regularity of a particular task. For example, when a student participates in doing his own laundry every Saturday at home, he learns that Saturdays are laundry days and stands a better chance of continuing this routine in his own living accommodation outside of the parents' home. Independent living skills (shaving, washing one's hair, bathing, money management, vehicle maintenance, medical appointments, etc.) should all be presented and practiced as part of a specific routine at home, from as young an age as possible. The more routines that can be established while a student is living at home, the more likely it is that the student will carry out those routines when living away from home.

LEARN TO PLAN FOR POSSIBLE CHANGE

As well as learning to structure time and create routines, one also needs to learn to tolerate change. Change is part of life, and it is a part of life that individuals with ASD universally struggle with, some more than others. In fact, small changes can sometimes wreak havoc. Parents and professionals need to help students adjust as changes occur. The bottom line is that no matter how well prepared they are, people with ASD will probably continue to struggle with change to some degree. To make things worse, one cannot plan for many of the changes that simply occur as part of daily life. However, students can learn about change as an unavoidable part of life, and can also learn self-soothing and coping strategies to help them tolerate change more adaptively.

Early preparation

There are many strategies that can be used to help students with change, and one can be very creative in this arena. One thing that always helps with any upcoming changes is to warn the student of the change in advance. It helps the student to know, for example, that a substitute teacher will be temporarily replacing his or her regular teacher. Social

Stories™ can also be used to facilitate the student's awareness and tolerance of upcoming changes and to help students understand the nature of change. Relaxation training and self-talk can be used (and must be practiced) to teach students to remain calm or to calm themselves down before their emotions escalate to a point of no return.

I encourage parents to desensitize students to changes gradually, in developmentally appropriate ways. Younger children can be provided with a visual schedule of activities for the day, with a blank space left after each one. The blank space is used to incorporate various other activities into the schedule, including some fun ones for the child. For example, if the schedule reads "dry cleaner"—"car wash"—"shoe store," parents can casually inform the child that they "forgot" to put a particular activity on the sheet and insert it between two of the other activities. The child can also be given an opportunity to add activities into the blank spaces if there is something she would like to do. In this way children feel included in the process. Parents should also be encouraged to periodically insert small but significant changes into any routines that are developed in the home. At first the child can be warned about the upcoming change, but unexpected changes should also be incorporated.

Later preparation

The recommendations regarding routines within the home should continue with older students. Although changes to the student's academic schedule, syllabus, and teachers can disrupt high-school and college students, they present important lessons in adaptability. Teachers need to know that if spontaneous changes are made in the general classroom without being specifically brought to the student's attention, there is no guarantee that the student will have noted or incorporated those changes. If changes are announced verbally by the teacher, the student may not independently recognize that adjustments to the syllabus need to be made. Therefore, any changes to the class syllabus should be provided to the student in writing, preferably personally, and the teacher must make sure that the student understands the change.

Students may have particular preferences or needs within the classroom environment. With regard to this, it will be important to develop self-advocacy skills in younger and older students by encouraging them to make specific requests on their own as much as possible. For example, Egan (2005) notes that in the college setting some students may insist on using a particular writing instrument, want to sit in the same seat for each class, or ask too many questions about assignments. A student who wishes to sit in the same seat could ask the Disabilities Services Officer to include this request in the letter that is developed for the student's professors. Ultimately, students must learn to take the initiative for making sure that their various needs are met within the classroom environment, when speaking with their professors for the first time. Students also need to take responsibility for having their preferred materials available, as well as a couple of suitable alternatives just in case. When these skills are developed before students leave high school, students are more likely to be able to advocate for themselves in college.

LEARN THE RULES OF MULTI-TASKING

Multi-tasking can be challenging for many individuals, not just those with ASD. Some people truly struggle when they have to multi-task, and they need to develop compensatory strategies, which ultimately may include finding a job that does not require multi-tasking. Multi-tasking can include working on many projects at one time while keeping track of all of them, taking notes while listening to a lecture, and following along with multiple conversations in a group of people.

Many students will need to have notes provided to them as an accommodation so that they can spend their time in class focusing on what the professor is saying. This is a commonly accepted accommodation (see Chapter 10). People who find multi-tasking easy are able to keep track of where they are on each project in their minds. Those who struggle in this area may find it difficult to manage multiple homework assignments and projects, and will benefit from keeping track of progress in a planner or on a whiteboard.

Early preparation

Young children can learn to make sequential charts for their various activities and routines (e.g. getting dressed in the morning, bedtime routine, etc.), as discussed above. They can also learn to make lists of things they have to do. The key point is to develop the ability to organize things in a sequence that makes sense and is easy to follow. As the child becomes better able to perform single tasks, he can be challenged to perform two tasks simultaneously. Using visual aids will always be valuable to students with ASD, so a two-step direction can be written out in words or pictures for the student to read while completing the task. Because sequencing is a cognitive skill in and of itself, I encourage parents and professionals to work closely with the child's educational team. In this way the entire team can be consistent in providing stimulating activities at the child's level of ability.

Later preparation

Learning to use a planner and a calendar will be essential for success in college. Planners can be used for multiple purposes: to plan what needs to be done, keep track of what has been completed, and identify dates when assignments need to be turned in. Some people make use of a large whiteboard divided into several sections (e.g. beginning, middle, and end). Multi-colored Post-It™ notes are used, designating one color for each project. The project is broken down into manageable steps that are written separately on a Post-It™ note. The notes are moved to the appropriate section on the whiteboard as each task is completed. I recommend that these skills be programmed into the student's educational plan from third grade and into high school. In elementary school students learn to use the basic system with one project at a time. Over the years they learn to break projects down into manageable chunks while managing more projects at a time. Students who struggle in this area will benefit greatly from specific instructional techniques and the assistance of an educational therapist or a specially trained teacher. Students who continue to struggle in the college setting may initially need the assistance of a mentor, tutor or coach for at least the first semester, and some for longer.

LEARN RESEARCH STRATEGIES FOR LIBRARY AND ONLINE RESEARCH, AND LEARN TO ORGANIZE RESEARCH FINDINGS

This is a skill that all students should learn throughout their educational careers. Most students will learn the basics of organizing research findings in high school. However, it is important to remember that students with ASD may not realize that the skill they are learning is not only important and specific to organizing research findings—it can also be transferred to other types of projects. Therefore, they will need specific instruction in the concurrent use of visual aids to outline the steps they need to take. It's also recommended that students practice the use of these visual aids in other projects.

Teachers and clinicians should examine the student's ability to generalize learned skills from one project to another. If the student struggles with generalization, visual supports can show him or her how skills learned in one project translate to others. These visual aids can become handy references for students throughout their educational career. Students who present with difficulties in the area of executive functioning will find organizing college-level research a bit more challenging, due to the vast amount of information available. This is another area where educational therapists, mentors, tutors, and coaches will become invaluable to the student with ASD.

Chapter 6

ASKING FOR HELP
SKILL SETS

After years of working with individuals on the autistic spectrum, it is very clear to me that one of the most significant problem areas for both children and adults is asking for help. It is uncanny how many adults I've come across that do not know how to ask for help. Younger individuals don't appear to understand when or that they need help. Once they recognize that they do need help, they are often unable to identify the appropriate individual from whom to seek it. This concerns one of life's most primitive survival mechanisms, yet we see so many individuals with autistic spectrum disorders (ASD) who struggle in this area.

Philosophically, the concept of living both independently and interdependently needs to be learned by both children and adults. As noted by Hoekman (2008), the idea of doing everything independently is misleading, as we all depend on others when faced with tasks we aren't equipped to do ourselves. For example, we usually depend on others when we need to get a haircut, for regular vehicle maintenance, and for maintaining aspects of our homes (e.g. electrical and plumbing), etc. Taking into consideration how literally many individuals with ASD understand things, it's important for them to know that both independence *and* interdependence are important skills to learn. Asking for help is multifaceted and involves a number of complex skills in the social, emotional, language, and cognitive areas. Some individuals truly believe that needing help is a sign of weakness. This myth can be dispelled by letting students know that asking for help is expected, especially in learning situations.

Poor communication skills may interfere in the ability to ask for help. All of the skills involved in asking for help can be confusing and, as such, may be avoided. Skill sets in this area can also be very abstract, which will challenge not only the student, but also the creativity of those developing intervention programs for students in this area.

UNDERSTANDING THE ROLE OF OTHERS IN ONE'S LIFE

The understanding that another person can be there for us if we need them is critical to one's sense of safety in the world. It is not only language based, but also grounded in the social and emotional concept of reciprocity—the give-and-take of relationships—one of the core issues in ASD. This is a complex area of development that will probably not come naturally to most people with ASD.

Early preparation

A classic example of challenges in this area is seen in young children on the spectrum who do not ask for help when they get stuck on a task or with a toy, or when another child takes something away from them. Most young children with ASD have to be taught to ask for help, and instruction in this area must continue throughout the student's educational program because the ability to ask for help as a child may not translate into asking for help as an older student or adult. Students must learn that willingness to ask for help is a positive attribute, and that teachers value students who ask for assistance and/or clarification.

Later preparation

Older students and young adults need to learn to rely on trusted others for assistance and information. For example, how do you find a good electrician, plumber, hair stylist, etc.? Most of us will intuitively ask a friend, relative, or neighbor for a referral, but this may not come naturally to people with ASD and/or it may pose developmental challenges. Older students who have received good foundational teaching in this area at an early stage will likely be more comfortable and resourceful when it comes to understanding the need and appropriateness of asking for help. Instruction will also need to be provided about how to identify appropriate individuals from whom to request assistance.

DEVELOPING A SENSE OF RECIPROCITY

Reciprocity is key to understanding the role of others in our lives, as well as our own role in others' lives. Any individual who receives a diagnosis of ASD will need intensive intervention in this area, starting in infancy (if diagnosis has taken place at so young an age), and continuing into high school and beyond.

Early preparation

Social reciprocity (e.g. turn-taking) and language reciprocity (e.g. conversation) can be developed in numerous ways, and a "no-holds-barred" attitude should be adopted when planning intervention in this area. Reciprocity should be expected, reinforced, and rewarded in all of the child's environments. In order for true reciprocity to be established, all therapists, educators, parents, and other professionals working with him should expect, reinforce, and reward reciprocity when interacting with him. In addition to traditional interventions, I recommend that role-playing, Social Stories™ and video modeling be used extensively at all ages to teach this important concept and develop awareness and ability in this area.

Later preparation

The type of reciprocity required of a young student is much less sophisticated than that which takes place between older individuals. Therefore, social reciprocity will need to be included in the student's overall programming through the high-school years and into adulthood. Reciprocity and relationships go hand-in-hand. Without relationships the student will not learn reciprocity. Adults without relationships will have no one to turn to as a resource for the type of assistance we all seek at one time or another.

KNOWING WHEN HELP IS NEEDED

Bliss and Edmonds (2008, p.94) wisely note that people with ASD (and even some without it) don't usually think "about how they do things right or how they get bad situations to go away." The notion of considering one's internal process when participating in a task, or when one gets stuck with a task, is important to develop in individuals who don't do this instinctively. Awareness of one's need for assistance is related to the cognitive skill of problem-solving. It also dovetails with self-awareness and self-advocacy, so without these skills, the student's growth and development in this area will be fragmented.

According to Gaus (2007), most people with AS "lack the prerequisite skill of *recognizing* their own internal mental states; *recognizing* that their distress can be a signal for a need to initiate a change in the environment; *differentiating* emotions from needs; and *translating* them into words" (p.158). The information processing deficits found in individuals with ASD are intimately related to executive functioning (EF) and play a significant role in how the individual processes experiences. Therefore, a combination of developing compensatory strategies for EF deficits and helping students develop the above-mentioned prerequisite skills will be important components of both the early and later preparation stages.

Early preparation

Younger students can role-play getting "stuck" and identifying potential helpers in different environments. Social Stories™ can be written to help students develop greater awareness about getting stuck and what to do about it. Video modeling of similar aged peers asking for help can be developed. Talk Blocks® (available from Innovative Interactions, LLC) can be used to help young students learn the basics of reciprocity, understanding one's emotions, and making requests to others. Talk Blocks® can be used to help children learn to express their needs and emotions. There are red ("I feel") blocks and green ("I need") blocks, each with 12 different options using pictures and words. By choosing a feeling block first and then a need block, children learn to identify their emotions and pair them with an act that can help them feel better.

Finally, stimulation of development in this area needs to occur in all of the student's environments: home, school, and community. It will also involve both formal and informal instructional methods.

Later preparation

As students get older, they can begin to identify what it feels like in their bodies when they get stuck or can't do something, and learn to take appropriate action in these moments. They need to learn to brainstorm solutions to problems and determine which of all of the possible solutions are the most effective ones. Physical and/or emotional states such as confusion, rage, apathy, or loss of focus can be used as cues for the student that she may need help, or at least that a change of some kind is necessary. Finally, helping students learn to recognize their internal states, and ultimately put words to them, will be key in the problem-solving process. As well as Social Stories™, Talk Blocks® for Work (available from Innovative Interactions, LLC) can help students learn to make connections between their internal states and the need for some type of action or change. By using the interactive block system, students select from "I feel" and "I need" blocks to facilitate the identification of emotional and physical states, and potential actions to help resolve the problem (Gaus 2007).

IDENTIFYING WHO TO ASK WHEN HELP IS NEEDED

The skill of asking for help will be essential throughout the student's education, and most certainly prior to the college years. Parents and educators need to push students to develop greater independence in this area, and students may appear to "resist." Because both communication skills and various aspects of EF are needed for effective functioning in this area, a good evaluation of the student's challenges in these areas will be important to identify deficits and skills that need to become more fluent.

Early preparation

Asking for help can be broken down into small, manageable steps that ultimately lead to independence in this area. It will be necessary to determine which aspects of this skill are difficult for each student. Can the student identify when she needs help? Once she has identified that help is needed, can she make the necessary subsequent decisions as to what to do next? For example, does the student know who, how, and when to ask for help? Often students with EF problems get stuck in the actual planning aspects of who to ask and how to go about asking for assistance. Different situations call for different helpers, and this is where students may become confused. They can practice these skills in various arenas, beginning by simply identifying an appropriate person to seek assistance from in a range of environments, asking a parent for help, asking teachers or other authority figures (e.g. store clerks, security guards, neighbors, etc.) for help, and finally, seeking assistance from peers when appropriate. Visual aids can be used in the form of a "help card" that sits on the student's desk. With some training, explanation and practice, students can learn to hand the card to a teacher or helpful peer any time they feel lost or confused, even if they don't know what kind of help they need.

It will be important to examine the student's thoughts, feelings, and ideas about what it means to ask for help. As already mentioned, asking for help is often seen as a sign of weakness. Some students feel uncomfortable asking for help because of a concern that the person being asked will feel "put upon" or taken advantage of. While skill development is important, these powerful beliefs can interfere in even the most adept student's ability to ask for help. Identifying these erroneous belief systems when students are young will ensure that the beliefs do not become more solidified in their world view, rendering them more difficult to change in later years.

Later preparation

As with many of these challenging skills, ongoing instruction throughout the high-school years will be essential to ensuring success as a young adult. Instruction in what to do and who to turn to when assistance is needed should be incorporated in the student's programming. Although not all situations can be predicted and planned for, students can learn to identify and keep a list of various people in their environment who would be appropriate to approach in various situations. Students can also select a "go to" individual for situations in which they cannot identify an appropriate person.

Some individuals will benefit from carrying a list with them that has the names of a few people and their contact information. It's been my experience in working with both children and adults that when they become highly anxious or confused, they often forget to use the "tools" we develop together. As one father reported, in spite of the amount of assistance that his son has received from the Disabilities Services program at college, he "doesn't always think to contact it" (Dutton 2008). My hope is that as this type of intervention becomes more strongly emphasized and integrated, beginning in preschool and continuing into high school, individuals with ASD will learn to use this strategy as if it were second nature. Because some students struggle with generalization, they may need to go through a conscious process of identifying appropriate "helpers" in all new environments, including the college setting.

Students with ASD need to know that asking for help is essential in college, and that colleges offer assistance in a number of areas. There are learning centers that offer tutoring, coaches may be available either through the college or in the community, peers can be of great assistance in many ways, and college professors encourage students to ask for clarification or assistance because they want them to succeed. Students will need to ask about each individual professor's preferences as to how and when to ask for help during class time. Most professors have office hours when students can come to talk face-to-face with them, or there is always the option to email professors with questions (Chew 2007). Befriending and setting up regular meetings with one's professors is a wonderful way for students to get assistance and clarification. Towards that end, students should keep a written record of each professor's office hours. The more the student is informed about where to go for various types of assistance, the better off he will be.

OBTAINING SOCIAL, EMOTIONAL AND SAFETY SUPPORT

Asking for help also extends into the social and emotional realms of life. Self-awareness will be key in helping students of all ages know when to seek support. Students will also benefit greatly from learning enduring rules about their own personal safety (see below for guidelines).

Early preparation

All of the suggestions mentioned in the self-awareness section (Chapter 2), dovetail with this skill. Young students need to learn to recognize and label their own emotional and bodily states, and strategies to use (including enlisting the help of others) when they cannot help themselves feel better. For example, one student started asking to use the bathroom whenever conversation was required (e.g. family dinners, group settings with peers, etc.). He would stay in the bathroom for extended periods of time because he was unable to express his confusion and discomfort about having to converse with others. This was his way of "escaping" the situation. His discomfort was multifaceted. He wasn't very interested in the conversation and didn't understand that these conversations helped families or friends feel closer to one another. He also didn't feel very skilled at making conversation. Finally, he preferred to read, or play a hand-held computer game, over engaging with others. After learning to identify what he was feeling in these situations, he recognized that he was using the bathroom to avoid the discomfort he felt. This is an excellent example of why it is so important to explore less adaptive behaviors with students in order to help them identify their struggles. This exploration process will also enable professionals and parents to understand the specific type of intervention needed. Once this student and his mother understood what was going on with him, he was better able to develop a broader skill base and learn ways to solicit his mother's assistance, rather than simply avoiding an uncomfortable situation. His mother, in turn, could be educated and feel better prepared for helping her son assimilate more effectively.

Later preparation

Students need to learn how to recognize signs of depression so that they can seek assistance before it's too late. They can learn about the various physiological, behavioral, and environmental cues that should alert them to seek support. With help from a therapist, the student can list various physiological cues that may be indicators of depression. Examples of these include: increased or decreased sleep or eating patterns, behavioral cues such as decreasing interest in pleasurable activities or falling behind in one's assignments, and environmental cues, including increasingly poor personal hygiene or falling behind in keeping one's laundry clean. This procedure can also be used to help students identify various signs of anxiety or stress.

Once students have learned to recognize various cues that signal the presence of these emotional issues, the concept of an "emotional toolbox" (Attwood 2007, p.159) can be developed with the assistance of a therapist. Together the therapist and student develop "tools" that can be used to alleviate depressive, anxious, and other negative emotions. Attwood recommends developing a number of tools in different categories, including: physical tools, relaxation tools, social tools, thinking tools, special interest tools, medication tools, and any other kinds of tools that meet the needs of the individual involved (Attwood 2007, pp.160–167). The toolbox is made as visual and tactile as necessary, and practice using the various strategies in the toolbox is strongly recommended.

When students feel depressed, anxious, or stressed out, they should not hesitate to make use of the counseling center, their private therapist, or at minimum their advisor. Social concerns can also be dealt with through the counseling center, one's advisor, or a local therapist. Many students will not know how to access on- and off-campus recreational activities, and will need guidance from peers, resident advisors, or other personnel. Other important areas in which students may need support are discussed below.

PERSONAL SAFETY

Students with ASD respond very positively to specific rules for different situations, and safety is one situation where rules can help to keep them safe. The best we can do is to help students develop a model for understanding their own reactions to potential danger, and provide them with possible options for when these reactions arise. However, it's important to keep in mind that not all potentially dangerous situations can be predicted or planned for. Here are some examples of rules that can be learned and practiced throughout the student's life in developmentally appropriate situations.

- If you're ever uncomfortable in a situation, or feel in danger, call parents or a specified trusted person.
- When out with a friend, always go to public restrooms together, even if you don't have to use the restroom.
- Keep away from poorly lit areas, and stay with groups of people. Avoid walking alone at night.

- Always ask who is knocking on your door before opening it, and if it's someone you don't know, don't open the door without a parent or trusted person around.

- Keep your door locked at all times and never let a stranger into your home. (This rule may need to be modified for dorm living, where students frequently leave their doors open.)

- Never give out any personal information (birth date, address, telephone number, social security number) over the telephone or on the computer, unless you know the caller very well (e.g. the caller is a personal or family friend). As students mature, they can learn more about computer safety and how to know when it's okay to use a credit card to make purchases on the internet.

- While we always recommend that children ask for assistance from police officers, security guards, or other people in uniform, they also need to know that whenever anyone (including these people) acts suspiciously, does something out of the ordinary, or makes you feel uncomfortable in any way, it's okay to excuse yourself and get away. While we'd like to think that we can trust all "official" personnel, wearing a uniform does not guarantee a person's goodness. Developing a repertoire of "escape clauses" for use in these situations will be extremely important for some students.

Finally, it will be important for students with ASD to understand their college's safety guidelines, including anti-hazing, prank phone calls, and anti-bullying rules, and how to get help, should anything of the kind happen to them or another student (Coulter 2003). (On college campuses, "hazing" is the process of initiating members into sororities and fraternities. Some of the various activities involved in hazing can be seen as abusive or humiliating.) They also need to learn how to deal with emergency situations, including how to contact emergency workers and how to deal with them. It is a good idea to program the phone number for the college's public safety division into the student's phone.

One way or another, it is important for the student to have someone they feel comfortable with to talk to (Chew 2007). It may take some time to identify the right person and develop a trusting relationship with them, so this should be a priority from as early on as possible.

Chapter 7

SELF-CARE SKILL SETS

Self-care is essential for a number of reasons. Hygiene contributes to the health and welfare of the self and others. It can also make the difference between social acceptance and rejection—most people are "turned off" by someone who is unkempt, dirty, or has body odor. Self-care also encompasses the broad area of independence in caring for one's financial, medical, transportation, and work/career needs, not to mention interpersonal responsibility. All of the skills in this area are incorporated into the concept of "independent living skills" (ILS). Skills in this area can be programmed in developmentally appropriate ways from as early as the preschool years. The importance of independence in self-care must be approached not only from a conceptual, but also from a practical standpoint. Self-care should be expected of the student in all environments. Toward this end, parents may need the support of a well-designed and supervised in-home behavioral program designed to develop and encourage ongoing independence, with concomitant strategies to deal with potential resistance.

TAKING CARE OF BASIC PHYSIOLOGICAL NEEDS AND HYGIENE

This is a skill that can be stimulated and developed from a very early age, keeping the ultimate goal in mind: that of recognizing, understanding, and attending to one's own physiological and bodily states including hunger, thirst, cold, heat, fatigue, need for sleep, need for exercise, basic first aid, and how to take care of oneself when not feeling well. Developing good, independently performed personal hygiene habits is a second component in this area.

Early preparation

Professionals and parents play an important role in facilitating the development of self-awareness in the area of physiological states, as well as in helping children develop basic self-care routines. Young infants cry when they are uncomfortable and/or hungry. Older students with autistic spectrum disorders (ASD) may need specific instruction in physiological awareness. Self-awareness techniques can help students learn to recognize the internal cues that correspond with various physiological needs (e.g. tummy growling usually means hunger; goosebumps usually mean one is cold). Students can then learn about various options for taking care of their needs. Parents may need to verbalize and use visual aids so that the child recognizes and understands different strategies for different needs (e.g. what to do for colds or fevers; how much sleep or exercise is needed to remain healthy; strategies to use when one has low energy, etc.). Parents will find that when self-care routines are developed and implemented as part of the family culture from the start, they will meet with much less resistance as the child reaches adolescence. Students should be expected to complete their own self-care with increasing independence and decreasing need for assistance or prompts. However, the use of visual aids can continue into adulthood. A number of books written for young children address the importance of taking care of their bodies, and these books can play an important role in the development of self-care.

Later preparation

I have been surprised to learn of many students who completely disregarded any one or more of their basic needs when they went to college, for a variety of reasons. Some students tell me that they "forget" to eat or drink; some go without eating because they don't know the cafeteria's hours of operation and don't make alternative plans if they miss meals. Some students have such a restricted diet, as a result of sensory challenges or because they follow a special diet, that finding food to eat in a cafeteria may be challenging. Using role-playing conditions in which students have to problem-solve various situations will be important. A number of different situations can be discussed, including what to do if the cafeteria is closed; what to do if the food in the cafeteria does not appeal to the student; finding alternative places to eat; what kinds of foods are good to keep handy in one's dorm room for snacks and possibly for small meals, etc.

Students who learn basic cooking skills while they still live at home will fare better when on their own. The entire gamut of skills involved in meal preparation should be learned, including meal planning, grocery shopping, and organizing foods in the refrigerator. Basic preparation, storage principles, and food cleaning skills should also be learned, including working with knives for cutting or chopping. Students can take a course at a community college or local park district, and families can also arrange for the student to prepare family dinners one or more nights each week, providing as little support as possible, but enough support at the outset while the student is learning. Keeping a shopping list of the student's favorite foods and other necessary food or cooking items on the student's computer is an easy way for the student to maintain and print out a shopping list when needed (Palmer 2006). Additionally, learning to clean various parts of the house (e.g. bathrooms, kitchens, etc.) and to use cleaning supplies and fluids safely is essential and should be incorporated into the student's general responsibilities or chores.

Personal hygiene can be an issue with adolescents in general, but teens with ASD who have not developed specific personal hygiene routines often struggle with their parents about this. This is why it is helpful to develop hygiene habits as a part of the family culture from very early on. Poor hygiene can result in social rejection and ridicule, and students who resist regular hygiene need to know about the social, medical, and occupational consequences. If the student is motivated to have friends or a romantic partner, hygiene will be essential, because no one wants to hang out with someone who smells, looks unkempt, or has bad breath. If students are not romantically motivated, discuss the impact of poor hygiene on teachers, peers, and future employers and colleagues.

To facilitate ongoing hygiene maintenance, Harpur, Lawlor and Fitzgerald 2004) recommend that students keep a running list of the types of cleaning supplies and toiletries they use. As supplies need to be replaced, this list can be used to create a shopping list. They also suggest creating a schedule for regular dental appointments, annual physicals, recurring medical appointments for medication or allergy management, etc. Since most individuals with (and many without) ASD are creatures of habit, forming consistent routines for all kinds of hygiene (e.g. bathing, washing hair, shaving, and brushing teeth; changing sheets; doing laundry, etc.) will make it more likely that these routines are incorporated into the student's daily or weekly program. In terms of self-care and safety, Palmer (2006) recommends providing students with a basic first-aid kit, along with specific instruction on how to treat various problems, including cuts, burns, and scrapes, and on appropriate use of first-aid items (e.g. antibacterial creams).

Individuals with ASD may have an altered sense of hot or cold. They may wear shorts and T-shirts in the winter or, conversely, multiple layers of long-sleeved clothing and pants in the summer. As long as the individual's health and welfare is not at risk, their personal preferences should be respected.

In addition to ongoing education in these areas throughout the student's life, it is helpful to provide them with a set of written rules that govern the care of their bodies. The high school health class introduces these concepts, and some students with ASD may need ongoing guidance to develop and sustain good self-care routines. Reinforcement outside of school can include discussion, visual supports in the form of charts or instructions in each of the above areas, discussion of ways to deal with potential problems, and actual practice. Students can take these visual charts or instructions with them to college. Some examples of instructions or rules are offered below.

- It's common for most people to eat three meals per day.
- Snacking on fruits, nuts, or other healthy foods is okay.
- If you miss a meal, you can get something to eat at a local diner or the grocery store.

- You can keep [list several items] in your room, just in case you get hungry or want a snack when the cafeteria is closed.

- Your body needs at least six to eight glasses of water per day. It's a good idea to bring a bottle of water with you to classes, because it may be hard to find water near each class.

- It's a good idea to get about eight hours' sleep at night. This gives your brain enough time to rest so that it can be alert and ready to learn the next day. Make sure you go to sleep at least eight hours before you need to wake up for class the next day.

- Go to the student health center when you don't feel well, when your body aches, when you have a temperature above 99°F, or if you've had a cold for more than one week.

ENVIRONMENTAL HYGIENE AND KEEPING PERSONAL BELONGINGS ORGANIZED

Environmental hygiene includes all aspects of keeping both public, shared space and private space clean and in order. Respecting others' belongings and their personal space is also intrinsic to environmental hygiene.

Early preparation

In the early years, emphasis can be placed on developing, implementing, and maintaining routines in the home and at school. Children should be expected to keep common areas of the home as orderly as possible. The use of visual aids in the form of pictures can help children learn where things belong. Sequence charts and visual reminders can also be used to facilitate greater independence in this area. Children can participate in organizing and managing their homework assignments, and it may be necessary to develop structured routines for turning in homework.

I discourage parents from "nagging" their child because this creates a dependence on external prompts. Students will benefit from learning strategies designed to help them remember to do things independently. The most effective approach for most families will be to develop a system in their home for when things need to be organized, put away or cleaned, and to stick to this schedule. A visual schedule can also be posted and, if necessary, the parent can remind the child about an imminent transition, which cues the child to look at his schedule to see what needs to be done next. I recognize that this will not be easy for parents, but it will go a long way towards reducing the child's anxiety about living independently and helping him to be successful in self-care.

Later preparation

The unique characteristics of ASD present interesting complications in this area. Individuals with ASD experience unique limitations in reciprocity and awareness of others—understanding the emotional states and needs of others and how their own behavior impacts others. The student with ASD needs to learn that environmental hygiene is important and *expected* at home and in their dorm room or apartment, and that it is *expected* that they maintain a basic level of organization for their personal belongings. Social Stories™ can address these expectations, including the social and emotional impact on roommates when one is careless about environmental hygiene. Students will also need to understand what to do if a roommate also has issues in this area.

As soon as students are old enough to handle cleaning supplies and equipment safely, they should be expected to participate in various aspects of cleaning: dusting, vacuuming, washing dishes, cleaning bathrooms, doing laundry, keeping belongings organized, etc. These skills are necessary for all students, whether they go away to college or live at home. It's been my experience that these skills are extremely difficult to develop when students stay home, probably for a number of reasons. Parents recognize that students can easily become overwhelmed, and parents have to make choices and pick their battles. As such, they may have chosen to battle over academics and not ILS. Educationally, students who are fully included in general education classes do not receive instruction in ILS as part of their school programs. Until recently, we have made the natural but inaccurate assumption that because these students are intelligent and high functioning (HF), they will naturally develop these basic skills, and so less attention and importance has been placed on developing ILS in these students. A significant gap may exist between students' academic abilities and their capacity for independent self-care. There needs to be equal emphasis on both if students with ASD are to become independent and self-sufficient.

Now that we have had an opportunity to see that high functioning students do struggle in this area, we can begin to develop ways to incorporate learning into students' various environments. Professionals who work with them must begin formal instruction in ILS no later than the beginning of high school, and ideally in middle school. Towards this end, philosophical and practical changes need to be adopted by the various service delivery systems. These changes should include formal intervention to develop ILS via the student's academic programming. Parents need to recognize the importance of incorporating ILS into the family culture. Government agencies that provide services to individuals with disabilities (see Chapter 9) need to modify their philosophies about when the provision of ILS will be granted. It has been proven time and again that deficits in ILS account for a significant percentage of failures in the college setting. Therefore, students need to be relatively fluent in this area if they are to be successful in college and beyond. I propose that school districts incorporate developmentally appropriate ILS programming, beginning in early elementary school and continuing through high school. I also recommend that families request specific in-home behavioral support programs to develop and sustain ILS skills, beginning when the child is in middle school and continuing until the end of high school.

TIME MANAGEMENT

Time management is a big issue for anyone who struggles with executive functioning (EF). Students need to learn how to develop and adhere to a schedule. I have already addressed some of these issues as they relate to homework and assignments. However, students also need to learn to manage their leisure time in relation to the amount of work they have, and this may be challenging.

Early preparation

Time management is a developmental skill that requires a degree of maturity that most younger students do not yet have. However, there are building blocks that can be introduced and practiced. The use of routines and schedules engenders good habits in young children and helps them learn that there is a time frame for completing activities. Professionals can help parents learn the many benefits of using a timer to help students in this (and other) areas. I recommend that parents use timers to eliminate power struggles over time frames—for example, to let students know when a transition is imminent. Activities, including homework and video game time, can be associated with specific lengths of time. Timers can be used for play dates and to help students learn to participate in non-preferred tasks for increasingly longer periods of time. In this way, young students begin learning the rudimentary aspects of managing their leisure time and incorporating less preferred, but important tasks that also need to be done.

Later preparation

The more independent a student becomes in determining his homework vs. leisure schedule while living at home, the more likely it is that he will carry this skill over into the college setting. By using the interventions and strategies described here, students can develop a higher level of independence in time and homework management. Parents should be less involved in structuring the student's homework time by approximately the seventh grade (if not before), depending on the student's maturity level. There are natural consequences to not finishing homework, and although parents don't want to see their child fail, it may be the only way for some students to recognize that they need to take responsibility. When parents adopt the non-interventional approach (ideally with the guidance of one or more professionals), they need to inform the student's educational team.

There is another very important reason why I discourage parents from getting too involved in their child's homework. Homework is a means for teachers to identify students who are struggling. When students turn in homework with no mistakes, a natural conclusion is that the student understands the material. Because special education services are only offered to students who demonstrate a need, insisting that students turn in homework with no mistakes can actually deprive their educational team of very important information and reduce the likelihood that they will receive specialized intervention.

Homework is usually not a "preferred" activity for most students. As such, homework in the more difficult subject areas will be particularly challenging. Using preferred activities as reinforcement for completing homework is one strategy that works, especially if it is implemented from the start, so that bad habits do not develop. Older students can be expected to employ time limits more independently (with the use of a timer), in the hope that this skill will be transferred to the college setting.

One issue that frequently arises in my work with parents is the student's "addiction" to video games. Video games can be used as reinforcement for active participation in homework. Students who have not been able to regulate the time they spend on their games should consider leaving them at home for at least the first semester. This gives them an opportunity to develop good time management skills without the potentially irresistible temptation of video games. While some students initially balk at this idea, after serious contemplation and discussion most of them ultimately agree to try it out. Again, any tools used in the student's academic and home settings should be transitioned into the college setting. Students should be given as much support as necessary to learn how to modify their schedules in this new environment. They will have much more free time in college than they did in high school and will need to learn how to accomplish less-preferred tasks during their free time.

MONEY MANAGEMENT

Managing one's finances involves a deeper understanding of money in the abstract. This includes having an awareness of "what banks do, what a checking account is, how a check translates into money, where the money comes from for an ATM, and the relationship between income and expenses" (Perry 2009, p.100).

Early preparation

There are several good books for parents on helping children develop good "money sense" (Bodnar 2005; Godfrey, Edwards and Richards 2006; McCurrach 2003). Although these books are not specifically written for children with ASD, they contain valuable suggestions that can be modified and implemented, starting at a young age and progressing into high school. Professionals can be instrumental in helping parents understand that the abstract concepts of money may not be easily understood by a child or young adult with ASD.

Money skills need to be incorporated into the child's programming as early as possible, and ongoing well into high school. Budgeting skills can be learned by having students divide their allowance into three separate accounts: one for their own daily use; one for purchasing special items for themselves; and one for birthday, holiday, or other gifts for family members and friends. In this way students learn to allocate their money, as well as the importance of remembering to include others in their plans. It is especially important to develop these skills before the age of 18, when individuals are legally considered to be adults. Many individuals with ASD tend to take their legal status quite literally. They struggle with the idea that according to the law they are "adults," yet they still have to be accountable to their parents for "their" money. Additionally, there are numerous reports of adults with ASD succumbing to financial scams and losing hundreds and even thousands of dollars.

Later preparation

In addition to understanding about the abstract aspects of money, it is important for students to learn how to budget their income and expenses, maintain and balance their checking accounts, and use ATM machines. Money management includes keeping track of one's expenses, paying bills, reconciling one's bank accounts, keeping to a budget and managing *what* one spends money on. Planning for independence in budgeting and financial responsibility will help students make good decisions and minimize stress in this area.

MANAGING MEDICATION

If a student takes any kind of medication, developing independence following the prescription, and learning how to obtain supplies, will go a long way towards reducing the chances of a medication crisis. Students who go away to college will have to find an appropriate pharmacy and learn when to call in for a refill. It is also imperative to help students plan on contingencies with regards to anything different from the way they take their medication at home, because individuals with ASD can be very rigid and often have difficulty with problem-solving. (See "Creating sameness and establishing routines" on pp.66–70). One important concern is that many students do not want to take medication and may stop doing so when a parent is not monitoring them. Clearly, this could have tragic consequences. If there is any doubt about the student's sense of responsibility in this area, it is important to engage a mentor or an advisor to check in with the student about medication on a regular basis.

Early preparation

I recommend that parents include the child in preparing her daily medication regimen by using a weekly pillbox which they fill together. Using a pillbox establishes an important routine, which can improve the student's compliance in taking medication later on, and is also helpful for students who have trouble remembering to take their medication. Parents will need to monitor their child's medication until compliance and consistency are achieved, because some medications can have potentially serious effects if not taken on a regular basis. I recommend that mental health practitioners working in this area get training in the benefits and side effects of the medications most commonly used in ASD. It's also important to work closely with the student's psychiatrist or referring physician when medication has been prescribed.

Later preparation

In addition to learning the ins and outs of taking prescribed medications, Palmer (2006) highlights the importance of teaching students how to use basic over-the-counter (OTC) drugs such as aspirin, ibuprofen, acetaminophen, and remedies for colds and allergies. OTC medications have their own risks, although many people do not realize this. Educating students about these risks, and also about the risk of combining OTC medications, could save a life. For example, many OTC cough and cold preparations contain acetaminophen (paracetamol), and taking excess acetaminophen is potentially harmful. Therefore, students need to learn to take medications according to the instructions and to read labels for warnings about drug interactions. Some OTC preparations contain alcohol, which could have implications for students who take prescription medications. It's a good idea for students who take prescription medication to consult with the prescribing doctor prior to taking OTC medication. Students who have specific medical issues that require regular use of prescription medication should keep an emergency card in their wallets for unexpected emergencies. The emergency card lists the student's identifying information, allergies, and medications/doses. Medical alert bracelets can be life-saving because emergency personnel are trained to look for them immediately when called to the scene of an emergency.

Most colleges offer health services to students, and it is recommended that parents purchase access to these services. Students who go to college away from home may need to find new health care providers to meet their specialized medical needs. There are so many new things happening at the beginning of the school year, and having to find a new doctor during that time would only compound the student's level of anxiety. I recommend that students meet with any new health care providers and practice getting to and from their offices prior to beginning classes. Students may or may not wish to sign an authorization for the doctor to speak to their parents. However, most students are willing to authorize limited contact relative to payment and general concerns. These are decisions that should be made in advance of classes and orientation so that the student feels comfortable calling on the doctor, once at school. Keeping this in mind, it's a good idea to set up as many new things as possible before school starts.

TAKING PUBLIC TRANSPORTATION

Learning the public transportation system in an unfamiliar setting can be a daunting task for any student. Students with ASD may need more specific instruction in this area, including access to visual schedules, knowledge about the routes and where the stops are, and exact costs, in order to feel as well prepared as possible. Minimizing stress levels in all areas will enable students with ASD to problem-solve or find assistance when things don't go as expected.

Later preparation

While this skill may not be relevant for younger students, they can still be exposed to public transportation by their parents. Older students should learn to take public transportation in their home town, even if they have a driver's license and a vehicle. Vehicles can break down, and having some familiarity with public transportation will help to minimize stress and anxiety in these situations.

MAINTAINING A PERSONAL VEHICLE

According to Coulter (2003), students should learn how to maintain their personal vehicles, where to go for repairs and maintenance, where to get gas, what the parking rules are for public streets and parking structures, and how to access roadside assistance. Students should also know what they need to do in case of a car accident. It is important to prepare students in advance, and to help them develop the tools they will need if ever they are faced with an emergency.

Chapter 8

SOCIAL SKILL SETS

Most individuals with autistic spectrum disorders (ASD) experience social isolation and rejection throughout their lives. Although it may appear that they prefer to be alone, in high school it is very common for students with ASD to report that they are extremely lonely. In a sample of college freshmen and sophomores, Jobe and White (2007) note that "individuals with a stronger autism phenotype (e.g., rigidity, preference for sameness, high attention to detail) report significantly more loneliness…and fewer and shorter duration friendships." The concept that people with ASD are "loners," which implies that they *prefer* to be alone, may not be completely accurate. Rather, after years of social confusion, rejection, and isolation it makes sense that an individual would fear taking a chance again, since confusion, isolation, and rejection during the formative school years can lead to avoidance— which further interferes with social learning and utterly compounds the problem. For many students, their parents are their only true friends, and sometimes staying home feels safer than venturing out into a world where they generally feel anxious and confused.

We still have a long way to go in helping students with ASD in the area of socialization. Many of the students I work with received early and ongoing intervention in this and other areas, from the age of three. Nevertheless, they still have a tendency to isolate themselves, in spite of feeling very lonely. Common fears are: rejection, not knowing how to start and keep a conversation going, inability to tell when someone has stopped talking and when it's okay to interject a thought, running out of things to say, inability to read nonverbal cues, misunderstanding and reacting inappropriately to sarcasm or jokes, and saying something stupid.

The good news is that current outcome research into social skills programs supports the benefits of participating in these programs for adolescents with high functioning autism or Asperger's Syndrome (HFA or AS). Sperry and Mesibov (2005) note that improvements in "self-confidence, independence, grooming and social communication" are a direct result of participating in social skills groups (p.374). Tse *et al.* (2007) describe a 12-week structured social skills program for adolescents where "moderate effect sizes on measures of social competence and problem behaviors were demonstrated" and both students and parents reported improvements on a number of standardized behavior rating scales (p.1967). Interestingly, the one area where benefit was not seen was in social awareness, and this may be where social skills training programs fall short. Social awareness is not a skill *per se*. It is a more psychologically based construct that is not easily "taught" and is built on other more foundational constructs, the most basic of which is self-awareness. Our task as professionals, then, is to develop ways to help students learn to know themselves. Once they can do this they will be better equipped to get to know others and understand how to interrelate with them. Toward this end, social support groups can be of great benefit if the group is structured so that participants give one another feedback about their reactions and demeanor in the group setting. These types of groups can begin in middle school and continue on throughout the college years.

Social facilitation groups should venture out to public places as a way of helping students practice their skills. Specific activities need to be designed. For example, a field trip to a specific event (e.g. a pumpkin patch, play, concert) can serve as a venue for practicing safety and other skills related to awareness of one's environment. Students could be divided into small groups and asked to complete various tasks, including: locate a security person and ask that person the way to the restrooms; find out how many children are present and how many adults, which might require asking a ticketing agent; take note of where the concession stands, restrooms, event entry doors, and exits are, and so on. Working in pairs or small groups builds in teamwork.

Exposure to various social settings prior to starting college will benefit all students. Nevertheless, there will be aspects of new social situations that, for individual students, may continue to be challenging. I recently met with a young man who graduated from a four-year university course and asked him to tell me about the most challenging part of starting college. He said that not knowing who he would see and where he would see them made being on campus stressful for him. In high school it's easy to predict, with some degree of certainty, who will be in your classes. In college new students arrive all the time. Also, there are numerous places on campus where students "hang out," and it takes longer to become familiar with who hangs out where. This can also make it confusing to set up a meeting place. In her interviews with a number of adults with ASD, Sicile-Kira (2008) discusses the heightened sensory challenges involved in meeting new people (e.g. the sound of their voice, their smell, their appearance), reinforcing the fact that "difficulties with social relationships were not due to just communication, but about the total sensory processing experience" (p.2). She goes on to note that sensory processing difficulties may also arise when adjusting to a new teacher or aide.

As we begin to understand how better to help students in the area of socialization, they will become more competent, and as a result should experience less rejection. Howlin *et al.* (1999) note that the most successful interventions for improving social skills include: the use of typically developing peers as mentors, role-play, drama, anxiety reduction, and video modeling. One of the most important things for students to learn is that their ASD will make socializing challenging for them, and that whatever difficulties they experience are not their fault (Dubin 2005).

The remainder of this chapter addresses some of the most challenging areas of social functioning that need intervention from an early age. The overarching goal of intervention in this area is to facilitate greater social comfort and assimilation in adulthood. Please note that in individual students there may be other areas that also require attention. It is my hope that the information in this book will be used by professionals and parents to develop relationship skills over the course of younger students' lives so that the next generation of individuals with ASD will meet with greater success in all of their relationships.

The skill sets presented below are highly complex. In all cases I will present a developmental overview of the skill set, and when appropriate I will present ideas for early and later preparation.

SOCIAL COGNITION

Many of the concepts that I've already introduced and will discuss further are related to the broad area of social cognition. Social cognition encompasses the cognitive and intuitive ability to understand other people's mental states and perspectives, including:

- awareness of physical states and emotions
- understanding cause-and-effect relationships in interpersonal situations
- understanding the senses and sensory processing
- identifying desires, likes and dislikes in oneself and others
- understanding the difference between knowing and thinking
- understanding different belief systems
- differentiating and understanding statements that include sarcasm or jokes
- understanding intentions and deception
- being familiar with the broad areas of cognitive and language processing, including pragmatic communication (see pp.21–22), Theory of Mind (see pp.23–24), and central coherence (see pp.101–102).

All of these constructs should be taught at developmentally appropriate levels throughout the child's primary and secondary education, during young adulthood, and in multiple environments. Integrating this kind of programming into multiple disciplines is key to developing a well-rounded knowledge base. For example, psychologists and other mental health providers typically address the social and emotional applications of these skills. Speech and language pathologists work on the language, pragmatic and social communication applications. Educational therapists and educators tap into the cognitive and practical applications. Behaviorists focus on the behavioral aspects of communication (e.g. eye contact, turn-taking, conversation scripts, etc.). This is not to say that any of these disciplines teaches concepts in isolation. There is a great deal of overlap between all of the disciplines' areas of focus. Therefore, coordination between all professionals on the student's intervention team is necessary to ensure that all aspects of instruction are covered. This interdisciplinary approach also enables professionals to plan opportunities for generalization of skills. Finally, a team approach can be a vehicle for professionals to learn from one another and to address roadblocks to learning as they occur.

FRIENDSHIP

The ability to form and maintain friendships is almost universally affected to one degree or another in individuals with ASD. Understanding the concept of friendship can also be difficult. Therefore, students often benefit from learning specific rules such as, "An acquaintance is not a friend. A girl who smiles at you is not your girlfriend" (Graetz and Spampinato 2008, p.2). Like other types of skills, friendship skills evolve throughout life. Assessing an individual's level of functioning is the first step in determining a course of treatment for moving that individual through subsequent stages. Attwood (2007) identifies four stages of friendship, and it is helpful to understand these in detail. For the purposes of this text I will summarize Attwood's stages, but I recommend becoming more familiar with Dr. Attwood's work in this area.

Early preparation

Attwood conceptualizes *Stage 1* as occurring between three and six years of age in typically developing children. At this stage the child's perception of friendship is based on two factors: "proximity" and "possessions." "Proximity" relates to other children who live close by or sit next to the child. "Possessions" relates to other children who have toys that are attractive to the child. As the child moves out of parallel play into cooperative play, friendship continues to be conceptualized in a more or less "egocentric" manner—a friend is someone who likes you or wants to play with you.

Stage 2 occurs between six and nine years of age. At this stage, children become increasingly aware that friends share mutual interests and that one needs a friend in order to play mutually interesting games. As the child's capacity for reciprocity evolves, emotional awareness also increases. Children begin to recognize others' feelings and the impact that their own behavior has on other people. Although friendships may evolve out of shared interests, a rudimentary awareness of personality develops as the child begins to recognize that friends enjoy one another's company. At approximately eight years of age the child appreciates that a friend is a person who one enjoys playing with, and also "someone who helps in practical terms (he knows how to fix the computer) and in times of emotional stress (she cheers me up when I'm feeling sad)" (Attwood 2007, p.72).

There are numerous intervention strategies that foster increasing growth and development in friendship skills. While typically developing children may *initially* learn about play from interacting with adults, children with ASD benefit from having adult play partners for slightly longer than would be expected in typical development. Via numerous varied and structured interactions with adults the child learns and practices important skills related to self-awareness, awareness of others, and reciprocity. Imaginative and pretend play can be fostered in structured ways, with a particular focus on expanding the child's repertoire of developmental themes (e.g. dependency, nurturance, assertiveness, conflict resolution, problem-solving).

Children learn more effectively when they engage in real-life experiences that have meaning for them. For this reason I recommend using naturalistic (but structured) play to develop skills in this area. Artificially structured activities may bring swift results, but the retention and adaptation of that learning to novel and spontaneous situations will suffer. Children who focus on specific scripts or play sequences or repetitive play will benefit when adults gently insert variety in order to gradually increase the child's repertoire and imagination. Social Stories™ can be used to help children understand various aspects of playing with others, including perspectives, emotions, reactions, and more. Video modeling can be used to teach new play styles, as well as to record the child's naturalistic play, and also role-plays. By observing the recording, children learn to evaluate the play and can practice making changes.

Most young children with ASD will need adult facilitation for increased social interaction during play dates and at unstructured times of their school day (e.g. free play and recess). Specific training and experience in working with students who have ASD is essential. Professionals play an important role in helping parents understand the importance of advocating for this support service at school and in the community.

Later preparation

Stage 3 of Attwood's friendship model develops between the ages of nine and thirteen. At this stage children begin to select friends who have specific, desirable characteristics, and they recognize that friendship also includes experience-sharing. As a result, children seek out friends with similar interests *and* values, as well as friends who exhibit caring and a need for "companionship." As the separation–individuation process unfolds, it is only natural for children to begin the move away from reliance on parents to reliance on friends for acceptance, opinions, and advice. Friends become confidants and are relied upon for support, protection, and mutual understanding. Children can learn a great deal from their friends about friendship, conflict resolution, and repairing relationships.

For the most part, gender becomes important at this stage, with typically developing children preferring friendships with same-sex peers. However, this doesn't always apply to individuals with ASD, for a number of reasons. Boys tend to have more typically developing female friends because young girls are more flexible and protective. They're willing to take a sweet, innocent boy under their wing and include him in their circle of friends. Most boys with ASD aren't interested in rowdy chase or athletic activities, and are more compatible with girls at this stage. Girls with ASD tend to prefer typically developing boys as friends, as their interests may differ from those of typically developing girls (e.g. dolls, fashion, the opposite sex, flirting, make-up, etc.). Most typically developing girls at this stage focus more on feelings and can also be quite competitive and unpredictable in their moods and loyalties, which can be too confusing for some girls with ASD. Although either gender would benefit from having friends of the same gender (and many do), a typically developing friend of the same gender generally has to be someone who is willing to play the role of a special mentor or buddy (Attwood 2007). This friend is the one who introduces the student to common trends and helps him or her blend in.

There are other important things that children learn from their same-sex friends, and children with ASD may not be privy to these lessons for several reasons, the more obvious of which is the tendency to prefer friends of the opposite sex, as noted above. Alternatively, the child with ASD may not learn the lessons that other children would learn simply by observation, deduction or implication. In fact, the child's naïveté will be obvious to most typically developing children, which often results in exploitation and/or mockery. Therefore, it will be most helpful for children to have specific, professional socialization training and supervision as appropriate. Throughout their school career, having a trusted adult or peer to turn to and consult with will be the most valuable gift anyone could offer them. I also recommend that there be a trusted person assigned to the student specifically for social and emotional support at college.

That said, I believe that individuals with ASD should also meet and befriend other people with ASD. As noted by Hand and Paradiz (2009), "Indeed, for those of us with autism, a first encounter with others on the spectrum is frequently one of immediate familiarity, a sense of finding one's own people" (p.9). All of us select friends and prefer to be with people with whom we have things in common. Parents understandably want their child to fit in by having typically developing friends. However, most individuals with ASD do not feel comfortable with typically developing people. We all need to feel a sense of belonging, and the only way to belong is through similarity and familiarity. People with ASD will probably have more in common with other people with ASD than with typically developing students. Interacting with "neurotypical" people can be confusing and anxiety provoking. In *Pretending to be Normal* Lianne Willey (1999) describes many experiences of pretending in order to fit in. However, not all people have the gift for pretence, and if they don't, they become the outcasts of the group, and they know it. Therefore, I recommend participation in clubs, organizations, or other venues where the individual's particular interest is what brings people together (e.g. chess club, science fiction, comic books, etc.). This is also an excellent way for college students to meet others with similar interests.

The teen's and adult's circle of friendships broadens during *Stage 4*, where friends begin to serve both multiple and individual purposes. Acceptance, compatibility, and similar world views become important in selecting friends. Attwood notes that self-acceptance is prerequisite to reaching this level of friendship. The capacity for self-reflection and the ability to understand another person's perspective are also prerequisites for attaining skills at this level, because this is when friendships become more intimate. Sharing thoughts and feelings is important at this stage and challenges in the area of social cognition can make it difficult for a student with ASD to relate at this level. Another important skill at this level is learning to distinguish between friends, acquaintances, and others who act "as if" they are friends but in reality are not.

Mental health professionals can play an important role in helping the student's parents and the treatment team understand the student's strengths and weaknesses in the area of friendship so that interventions are developmentally appropriate. Initial programming must focus on developing the prerequisite skills discussed above, in multiple environments. Students need to learn how to evaluate other people in order to determine whether they share common interests and values. It will be important for students to learn to identify and understand what others expect of them and whether or not they feel uncomfortable, threatened, afraid, or confused when associating with a particular person (Harpur *et al.* 2004). This kind of learning can minimize the risk of being victimized. Students need to understand that conversation is not simply for sharing information about a particular interest. Conversation "is also a means of getting to know someone and letting him or her get to know you" (Harpur *et al.* 2004, p.128). Teaching conversation skills will be important, but specific instruction on how to gather information from another person by way of conversation is essential for the student with ASD.

Much of this can be learned via role-playing and structured activities where students learn to interview one another and subsequently share what they learned about the other student. Students can also interview teachers or family members for additional practice. It is helpful to videotape these role-plays because, more often than not, they will be able to see what they might have missed. Video modeling and talking about short scenes in television programs and from passages in books can also be used towards this end. Finally, structured social skills programs can stimulate social learning. In these groups students learn how to initiate and sustain friendships, and the relationships students forge in social skills groups often become long-term friendships.

At all stages of developing friendship, students with ASD will have to learn specific rules for appropriate interaction with others. Instruction in maintaining appropriate boundaries (e.g. how close to stand, rules for appropriate touching, appropriate topics) and pragmatic communication (e.g. eye contact, maintaining topics, reading the listener's cues, etc.) are important starting points. Harpur *et al.* (2004) offer numerous important "tips" about conversation, including: distinguishing between talking *at* and talking *to* peers; turn-taking as one of the most important building blocks of conversation; and making sure to not avoid making occasional eye contact with the listener. They talk about conversation as being a "language game" that incorporates a number of moves, including initiating moves (i.e. starting the conversation); acknowledging moves (letting the speaker know you heard them in one way or another); signals to let the listener know you're finished; and waiting for your next turn. In order to be able to sustain conversations students need to develop good listening skills, and also learn to read nonverbal signals. The use of gestures will help the listener stay connected to the speaker's words, and the role of body language must also be understood. Appropriate use of eye contact, or an appropriate way to let the listener know that the student struggles with eye contact, will also be useful skills to develop. Finally, Harpur *et al.* point out that "communication is emotionally loaded" (p.167), which accounts, in large part, for the individual's life-long struggle to interact with others.

READING BODY LANGUAGE AND OTHER NONVERBAL CUES

Body language, nonverbal cues, and tone of voice are essential aspects of communication, and deficits in the ability to understand these subtle forms of communication can result in confusion and misunderstanding.

Although this skill develops innately in most people who are not on the autistic spectrum, individuals with ASD truly struggle to understand and integrate the meaning of gestures, body postures, and facial expressions during an *in vivo* encounter, in spite of the fact that they may be able to identify these characteristics individually. Most structured psychosocial and speech and language intervention programs focus extensively on these skills. Some students will experience success in this area during individual therapy sessions or even in small groups, but will struggle with generalization of learning to other environments. Building practice and familiarity with learned concepts into activities in different settings may be the only way to address this challenge.

In addition to role-playing and video modeling, I've found it useful to watch soap operas or sitcoms with my clients, but with the sound turned off. The goal of this exercise is to identify how characters are feeling, what they may be communicating based on their body language and facial expressions, and what types of behaviors or interactions cause one or more characters to react in specific ways. A follow-up conversation about how these experiences manifest in the client's family or other relationships can also be useful.

Another key area of focus is to help individuals examine their own body language and develop an understanding of how others might interpret their gestures, body postures, and facial expressions. Individuals with ASD are frequently reported to use fewer facial expressions and gestures, and they may speak in a rather flat or monotone voice. This paucity of expression can be misinterpreted to mean that the individual with ASD is uninterested or bored. It's not uncommon for individuals with ASD to have overall weak muscle tone, and weakness in the facial musculature can account for flatness in facial expression.

Young adults will need to find a way to acknowledge their differences in nonverbal communication to avoid this type of misinterpretation. Attwood (2007) suggests that individuals consider providing an explanation for specific characteristics that may be confusing to others. For example, when going on an interview, an individual who struggles with eye contact can let the interviewer know that although she may not be looking at the interviewer, she is in fact listening, and that looking away helps her concentrate on what the interviewer is asking or saying.

Intervention in this area should begin as soon as an individual is diagnosed. Many of the children I work with come in and out of treatment, depending on the issues in hand. It is not uncommon for me to work with a young child until skill levels are developmentally consistent with the child's social and emotional level. Note that I did not say "developmentally consistent with the child's chronological age." This is an important distinction. We cannot expect individuals to perform tasks that go beyond their developmental capacities. For example, I worked with a child who was 12 years old but her developmental abilities and play skills fell somewhere in the five- to six-year range. The child's parents wanted her to be fully included in middle school so that she would "learn" to play from her typical peers. It was difficult for them to understand why I disagreed with them, until I asked if they would put their typically developing five-year-old child into a middle school setting. Development in all areas progresses along fairly predictable lines. Working at the child's developmental level—wherever that might be, and regardless of the child's chronological age—will elicit greater success and can help the child's parents understand and relate to their child in more meaningful ways. Indeed, parenting a HF child with ASD can be challenging. The child's academic and cognitive abilities likely fall within the average to above average range, but his or her emotional development is delayed by two or more years. The challenge parents face is how to interact and deal with an individual who is chronologically one age, but developmentally much younger.

EMPATHY

A common myth about individuals with ASD is that they are not empathic. This myth evolved, in part, out of a misunderstanding or misinterpretation of differences in individual expression, which brings to mind a very important issue in working with all kinds of clients. Just because an individual doesn't react in a manner that is common, expected or familiar to us, doesn't mean that the individual doesn't experience the *feelings* that accompany normal reactions. This issue is addressed by Dziobek *et al.* (2008) in their study of cognitive and emotional empathy in adults with Asperger's syndrome. The authors note that neurotypical individuals' "emotional reactions to others in distress often include *behavioral* reactions such as change in facial expression (e.g., sympathetic look) or helping behavior (e.g., consoling)" (p.471). As a result of the biological aspects of the disorder (e.g. impoverished facial affect and social anxiety, among others), individuals with ASD may not exhibit facial expressions or helping behavior in the same manner. As such, their reactions may be perceived as less intense, or perhaps even absent. However, these researchers found no differences in the *experiencing* of emotional or affective empathy between the Asperger's and control groups in this study. Differences did occur between the two groups in the area of cognitive empathy, "or the capacity to take the perspective of another person and to infer their mental states" (p.464). This capacity is associated with Theory of Mind, an area in which individuals with ASD are known to have impairments. The authors note that deficits in cognitive empathy may contribute to differences in reactivity seen in individuals with ASD, who may misinterpret, misread, or misunderstand mental states.

People with ASD have uniquely distinct reactions to emotional experiences. At times they may exhibit what would typically be classified as overreactivity (e.g. rages, tantrums, obsessive focus on an experience, etc.), while at other times they may appear to be highly underreactive to experiences. For example, an individual may react "inappropriately" (e.g. laughing in situations where crying is considered more appropriate). There are many reasons why laughter erupts in a highly charged emotional situation. Sometimes intense emotional experiences elicit uncontrollable laughing, even when the individual doesn't experience the situation as funny. Therefore, the meaning or intensity of an individual's reaction can only be determined after exploring the emotional experience underlying it.

People with ASD can also differ in the way they express feelings of grief or loss. The individual may exhibit sadness, but parents commonly report that the sadness is of significantly less intensity and duration than would normally be expected. As a result, parents often fear that their child lacks empathy. However, when talking with individuals about loss, it becomes clear that they feel loss very deeply. Older teens and adults may see death as the logical and expected end to life. Consequently, they may not see the "need" to mourn extensively, but not because they don't experience loss.

Taking the above concepts into consideration, empathy constitutes an extremely broad area of learning for students with ASD. Instruction in Theory of Mind, perspective taking, understanding emotions, and reading body language is essential for learning about and experiencing empathy. Students need to learn a variety of ways to demonstrate empathy. They also need to understand that diminished behavioral expression may be mistaken for lack of empathy. In cases where behavioral expression is difficult for whatever reason, students can learn various verbal expressions to convey understanding and empathy. While instruction in empathy needs to begin from the time the student is diagnosed, many of the skills involved are more likely to be consolidated and enacted when individuals are older and more mature.

CLASSROOM ETIQUETTE

Students with ASD may need specific instruction in classroom codes of conduct at the primary, secondary, and post-secondary levels. Some of the challenges students have in this area include learning to raise one's hand, waiting to be called on before speaking, limiting the number of questions asked, learning to inhibit one's desire to correct the teacher, and understanding the subtleties of how to disagree with teachers and peers. Understanding how much participation is expected, or when is a good time to interject an idea, can be confusing to many students with ASD. Therefore, expectations about classroom participation should be conveyed directly to students. Many students benefit from creating a chart or keeping notes to help them remember the expectations and rules of each class.

Social hierarchies can present an additional challenge. I've worked with students who simply cannot accept the inequity of professors asking to be addressed as "professor" or "doctor," while addressing students by their first names. When these types of issues arise, I validate the client's observation that there is, in fact, a hierarchy that may be unfair. However, the hierarchy exists, and if they insist on challenging it, their professors will likely consider their insistence adversarial.

MANAGING ONE'S EMOTIONAL REACTIONS TO THE COLLEGE, PROFESSORS, AND PEERS

All students experience intense, negative reactions to their school, teachers and/or peers at one time or another. Students who have negative experiences in school for whatever reason (e.g. feeling misunderstood, isolated, picked on, or bored) may inaccurately attribute memories of these negative experiences to all schooling in general. For example, negative experiences in grade school or high school may lead the student to assume that college will simply be more of the same. Similarly, students who have negative experiences in college may opt to drop out and discontinue education as a result. Grandin (2004) notes that mistakes and faults tend to disrupt the sense of balance that people with ASD long for, and that they have a tendency to focus on these. If this happens, students will need help identifying the positive and negative aspects of their experience in order to recognize that not all parts of it were bad (if that is true). "Black or white" thinking, difficulty considering alternative possibilities, rigid thought processes, and fear of going through another negative experience may make it difficult for the student to understand that all experiences have the potential to be positive, negative, or neutral.

It is not uncommon for interpersonal problems to occur between students and their professors or peers. Letting students know that this is "normal" helps them feel less embarrassed or confused when they have these experiences. One of the challenges of going away to college revolves around learning to deal with different personalities without the comfort and familiarity of home. Problems with roommates are quite common amongst freshmen and sophomores in college. Although it may not sound like a big deal, it is, and it can have a significant effect on students, whether they have a disability or not. Students should have a trusted contact person (e.g. a mentor, advisor, resident advisor, therapist, etc.) who can help them manage these (and other) situations. In summary, the ability to consider and identify the positive and negative aspects of their experiences and relationships is essential to developing an increased capacity to tolerate adversity.

RECOGNIZING WHEN YOU'RE BEING TAKEN ADVANTAGE OF AND PROTECTING YOURSELF FROM EXPLOITATION

Social and interpersonal naïveté and a strong desire to belong, fit in, and have friends makes individuals with ASD particularly vulnerable to exploitation and victimization. Often students with ASD have no choice but to befriend any group of other students who will accept them, and often they are "befriended" specifically to be exploited. Because of their propensity to tell the truth, many individuals with ASD become extremely upset by injustice and by being wronged. For many, it's even difficult to accept that people do lie, deceive, and exploit.

Early preparation

Initial preparation involves developing the ability to recognize basic facial features. Subsequent preparation includes learning to recognize the features and body language of deceit. However, this does not guarantee that students will recognize deceit when it is happening to them. Social Stories™, role-play, video modeling, and anything else that one can creatively conceive of will be essential in helping students develop awareness that not all people are honest. Activities that focus on developing trust and identifying trustworthy individuals will also be beneficial. Self-awareness is key here, in that students need to learn to be cautious when making new friends, paying attention to their bodily reactions to other people. Any uncomfortable feelings need to be understood as a signal to exercise caution. The other crucial area of focus is Theory of Mind. Learning how to take another person's point of view will enable students better to understand why it might benefit someone to be dishonest (e.g. for personal gain).

Later preparation

Role-play designed to challenge students to problem-solve specific situations is an excellent strategy to use with older students. As students are cognitively able to learn and understand the rules of friendship, they can begin to decipher what is appropriate behavior between friends. However, they also need specific instruction in what is *inappropriate* behavior and how to tell if someone is engaging in questionable practices with them.

Students with ASD may not be able to identify inappropriate behavior without specific instruction in what constitutes it. This poses a significant instructional challenge because there is no way to predict the various types of inappropriate behavior that students might encounter. Furthermore, poor generalization of learning may continue to put the student at risk. Harpur *et al.* (2004, p.77) recommend teaching the concept of "false friends" as (for example) individuals who borrow things but "forget" to return them, or individuals who ask to stay with you until they find another apartment "but 'forget' to pay their rent or buy food." They also note that it may not be easy to safeguard from false friends. Having a trusted individual with whom the student can address friendship concerns, or who checks in with the student about current friendships, is one way to safeguard students from exploitation and victimization.

SEX EDUCATION

Three things that need to be made very clear to individuals with ASD during sex education are: without contraception, sex will likely result in pregnancy; without protection, sex can result in the acquisition of a sexually transmitted disease; and the use of contraception and protection is mandatory until one is ready to start a family. Education about contraception and safe sex is essential for this population, because they may not necessarily learn it from their peers. They may also get misinformation from their peers and not realize it.

Sex education should ideally occur before the individual becomes sexually active. This is an area that many parents avoid, perhaps because of their own values, the child's developmental level, and their own fears about their child's safety in sexual encounters. However, looking the other way for whatever reason will not deter students from sexual exploration or prevent sexual exploitation. Parents can work closely with the child's treatment team to identify the best time and manner in which to approach this subject. There are also a number of very good resources available for parents and students (see Attwood 2008, for example).

LEARNING EXPECTATIONS ABOUT DATING

Dating can be a confusing venture for people on the autistic spectrum. Women with ASD can experience rejection because they may not fit the traditional image of females promulgated by our culture as it pertains to fashion, looking feminine, and being nurturing. This is not to say that women with ASD are not feminine or nurturing, but they often don't fit neatly into the feminine stereotype represented in the media. Faherty (2002) notes that women on the autistic spectrum may feel societal pressures to get married, or to dress or act in a specific manner that may not be consistent with how they feel or perceive themselves. Sexual victimization is also common in females with ASD. I've worked with several adult females who were either sexually victimized as children or raped as adults as a result of their inability to understand deception, to assert themselves firmly, or to call out for assistance. Several of the younger girls I work with are unable to say "no" to anyone for *any* reason, and as a result are at high risk for victimization. One ten-year-old client begged her parents for a dog because she felt that a dog could protect her from "mean" people. Some men with ASD can be seen as over-zealous in their attempts to woo a woman. To some women this can feel like stalking; others may feel flattered by being pursued so intently. Interestingly, this is often one of the first characteristics that many neurotypical women cite when asked what first attracted them to their spouse who has ASD. Other men with ASD can also appear shy and/or immature when it comes to wooing a woman.

Early preparation

Early preparation in this area involves learning about friendship and how to protect oneself from exploitation, as described above. Role-play can facilitate the child's ability to understand deception and increase her comfort level with saying "no" and seeking adult assistance. Developing friendship awareness and discrimination skills between who is, and who is not a friend, as well as grasping the concept of "false friends" mentioned above, can be done by way of Social Stories™, friendship groups, and other didactic and *in vivo* experiences. Younger students can also begin learning how to get to know someone at deeper levels by developing good communication and listening skills. Often young students will misunderstand the need to delve into more personal areas in order to get to know someone better. At times they consider simple questions such as, "What school do you go to?" as being way too personal.

Barriers to deepening relationships can be explored early on, opening the door to fuller personal and interpersonal exploration and disclosure. Getting to know another person's interests and abilities is one level of friendship, but getting to know that person's feelings, conflicts, values, and ideas takes a friendship to a more meaningful and intimate level. Younger children should also learn to notice important details about other people. This skill, in turn, enables them to learn when and how to give compliments.

Later preparation

Developmentally appropriate education about sex, issues of sexuality, and dating needs to take place before students go to college. Therefore, it will be important for students to participate in social skills groups with a focus on these issues throughout high school. Support in these areas may also be needed in the college or work setting, because students with ASD have trouble generalizing previous learning to new situations. Social skills groups in the college setting should reinforce social and sexuality learning and include education, role-play, and, whenever possible, *in vivo* learning. For example, a student mentor can help teach how to approach another student in the cafeteria, at the library, in the dorm, and in many other school environments (VanBergeijk, Klin and Volkmar 2008).

One of the most commonly reported challenges related to dating is learning (and accepting) that "no" means "no." I know many elementary and high-school students who have trouble understanding when another student is not interested in them, romantically or otherwise. The student of interest can become one of the student with ASD's restricted interests and, as such, may come to feel "stalked" by the student with ASD. In these situations significant rejection of the latter occurs, and because he or she cannot read the other student's nonverbal cues, the pursuit continues. At times the student with ASD believes that if he changes his behavior, the other will want to spend time with him. Social Stories™ and strict "rules" about not having contact with the pursued student are often necessary in this situation. If there is a trained professional at school who can intervene, they can meet with both students and share the desired student's perspectives with the student with ASD. Learning to understand friendly vs. unfriendly social cues, interested vs. uninterested body language, tone of voice, choice of words, and reciprocity are just some of the many skills involved in selecting an appropriate, interested friend and mate. In general, it is important that students learn to respect "the rights and entitlements of members of the opposite sex… When one student tells another student that he or she is not interested in dating, this decision must be respected…no matter how disappointing this is" (Harpur *et al.* 2004).

Most initial contacts with others will likely begin with "small talk," and often individuals with ASD do not enjoy, understand, or know how to engage in small talk. These types of conversations serve as "ice breakers," and if one is unable to manage them, it may be difficult to find common ground that could later lead to deepening a relationship. Because individuals with ASD are so adept at conversing about their favorite topics, Shore and Rastelli (2006) recommend learning when and where to initiate conversations about various topics. They suggest talking about special interests only in settings where others share those same interests (e.g. clubs). However, they recommend waiting until someone else brings up the topic. They also suggest keeping track of a few important facts or characteristics about new people that can later be used to initiate or enhance conversations. Finally, they recommend learning how to allow others opportunities to share their own thoughts during conversation. In summary, individuals with ASD will benefit from learning active listening skills, reciprocal conversation and pragmatic communication skills, and how to share emotions and desires within the context of a relationship.

Learning to distinguish if someone is romantically interested or is simply being friendly is an important skill. In many relationships one individual may experience romantic inclinations before the other, and/or one person may never feel romantic inclinations towards the other. Challenges in reading social cues and understanding others' emotions or perspectives can significantly interfere in this process. A few good ground rules can help the individual with ASD.

- Romantic relationships usually start out as non-intimate friendships where two people share common interests and activities. Even if someone is not romantically interested, that person can still turn out to be a very good friend. Small talk and inviting someone to join in an activity of mutual interest (e.g. a movie or an art exhibit that both parties are interested in) provide an opportunity for both individuals to get to know each other better and identify commonalities without the added pressure of romance. Multiple opportunities for shared experiences create a foundation from which a more romantic relationship can evolve.

- Internet dating, email, and chat rooms are ways to "meet" people in an arena that may be more comfortable for individuals with ASD. Internet dating can be somewhat less stressful for the student with ASD because there is a sense of control over the criteria used to select a person. It also eliminates some of the anxiety associated with interacting face-to-face with and being rejected by someone (Harpur et al. 2004). Be cautious when inviting a relative stranger out for a number of reasons. A good rule of thumb when asking an online acquaintance to meet in person is that several "conversations" about shared interests have taken place, and there is a comfort level between the two people. For safety purposes, always arrange a first date or meeting in a public place. Students also need to know that people are not always truthful in the way they present themselves on an internet profile. It may be a good idea to have support when looking at profiles, and also when putting together one's own profile for an internet dating service or social networking site (e.g. Facebook).

- Meeting someone you've never met before in person can be anxiety-provoking, especially because there is no way of knowing whether either party will feel comfortable. Therefore, it is safer and more appropriate to plan on keeping these types of meetings short, with activities that lend themselves to short meetings (e.g. coffee or lunch, rather than a movie or an exhibit). In this way, both parties know that it is acceptable to dismiss oneself politely after a short time without disappointing the other person too much.

- Being turned down is common and should not immediately be misconstrued as complete lack of interest or rejection. Shore and Rastelli (2006) recommend following the "three strikes" rule, which simply means that if the same person has turned down an invitation three times, it's likely that they are not interested in pursuing a friendship or romantic relationship. In these situations it is wise to move on in order to avoid being thought of as a stalker.

According to Attwood (2008), individuals with ASD also need to learn the difference between appropriate public and private behaviors. Additionally, getting consent at every level of romantic advance is essential. It will be useful for individuals to learn the various stages of physical intimacy, what types of feelings are associated with each stage, and at what point in a relationship each type of physical intimacy is appropriate. Both individuals in the relationship need to feel comfortable at all times, and should feel free to express their feelings when they are not. *"No" means "no!"* This is an absolute rule for which there are no exceptions.

Finally, I recommend that professionals in the field of ASD use Knapp's stage model of relationship development (Knapp 1978 and Knapp and Vangelisti 2005, as discussed in Guerrero, Anderson and Afifi 2007) to educate individuals with ASD on the various stages of closeness and intimacy. Here are a few basic guidelines for developing physical and emotional romantic attachment.

- Friends do not touch romantically. They may give one another a hug and/or brief kiss on the cheek as a greeting or parting gesture, but otherwise there is no touching at the friendship level. These behaviors are always acceptable in public areas.

- After several official "dates" or when it feels comfortable to both parties (which may require a conversation about comfort levels), holding hands and/or placing one's arm around the other's shoulders or waist may be appropriate. These behaviors are not offensive and can be exhibited in public with mutual consent. However, if one party initiates holding hands or placing an arm around the other and the other moves away, the gesture of moving away means "no."

- The initial romantic kiss usually occurs next, and also requires mutual consent. Although many couples kiss briefly in public, extended displays of romantic kissing are unacceptable in public. This is where the expression, "Get a room!" comes from. Couples in the early stages of their relationship may have a hard time avoiding romantic kissing in public. However, kissing is a very intimate, private experience and sharing it in public can be uncomfortable for some people.

- From the initial romantic kiss, the couple can proceed to the flirtatious touching of one another's bodies over clothing, sometimes referred to as "petting." The time frame for beginning this phase of intimacy is different for every couple. For some couples, several months go by before progressing to this level. Touching someone sexually is never okay in public.

- This flirtatious touching progresses to "heavy petting," which consists of touching underneath the clothing. Heavy petting is also referred to as "foreplay," which is usually a prelude to intercourse, or making love. At this stage the couple mutually consent to all levels of touching, with and without clothing. Once again, this level of sexual intimacy is never okay in public.

- Making love (intercourse or sex) usually occurs between two people who truly feel close to one another and who have been in a relationship for a significant period of time. Some people believe that sexual intercourse is only appropriate between a husband and wife. The couple will have accumulated an array of shared experiences that provide a foundation of trust and caring. Many people report that there is a big difference between "making love" and simply "having sex." Making love occurs between two people who feel very close to one another, who treat one another respectfully and kindly, and who share a great deal of themselves and their feelings with one another. Making love is not considered casual sex. Casual sex *does not* necessarily involve strong, romantic feelings toward the other person. However, casual sex can complicate a friendship and give rise to confusing feelings. As a result, if one or the other person in a friendship is not interested in a romantic relationship, it probably isn't a good idea to enter into a casual sexual relationship, because there is a risk of losing that friendship. Sexual intercourse is not considered to be appropriate in public.

There are three final areas of relationship learning for students with ASD: What constitutes a romantic relationship besides physical intimacy? What do partners in a romantic relationship expect from one another in order to sustain the relationship? What happens when one partner wants to terminate the relationship? Although I've touched on some of these issues throughout this section, they merit further exploration because they represent some of the strongest core challenges faced by individuals with ASD.

What constitutes a romantic relationship besides physical intimacy?

It's not uncommon for people to misconstrue sexual desires and physical intimacy as entirely representative of a romantic relationship. However, there is more to being in a romantic relationship than physical intimacy, and without these important factors, the relationship will likely not last. First and foremost, there must be a sense of shared love and respect for one another. For most couples, this means not just feeling love and respect, but expressing it to the other person by one's actions, and also verbally. Many neurotypical partners of people with ASD experience a strong sense of loss in this area. So what are some of the small things that sustain a relationship?

- Making an effort to remember and honor birthdays, anniversaries, and other special occasions.

- Verbal expressions of love.

- Complimenting one's partner about the way they look, something they did, an act of kindness, personal and/or professional accomplishments and endeavors, etc.

- Communicating simply to touch base with one another, on a daily basis (e.g. calling just to say "hi").

What do partners in a romantic relationship expect from one another in order to sustain the relationship?

Although this question appears quite similar to the previous one, these expectations are not just "small things." They are the foundation of what keeps a relationship strong and helps both people feel connected and supported:

- Being available to talk about emotions, conflicts, or upsets, whether related to the couple or otherwise.

- Knowing that each partner will share his or her own perspectives about emotions, conflicts, or upsets in an effort to help the other person formulate good and healthy solutions.

- Having the sense that your partner would do anything for you, even if it meant sacrificing his or her own unique interests for whatever length of time was required.

- Developing a sense of shared actual and shared emotional experiences that perpetuate the emotional bond and sustain an enduring sense of being within the relationship.

What happens when one partner wants to terminate the relationship?

After extended periods of not having one's needs met within the context of a relationship, the partner who feels the loss can react in a number of different ways. For example, the partner might reach out for communication; become frustrated, angry, or sad; isolate, avoid or withdraw; and ultimately want to terminate the relationship. If the couple can communicate about what is happening, it may be possible for the relationship to survive, but if not, it will ultimately end. In couples where one partner has ASD, that partner often feels befuddled and lost when it comes to the demands of his or her neurotypical partner. Psychotherapy with a mental health practitioner who specializes in ASD can be instrumental in creating change within any relationship if both partners are motivated.

LEARN HOW TO ENCOURAGE WANTED AND DISCOURAGE UNWANTED ADVANCES

Shore (in Shore and Rastelli 2006) describes the challenges he faced in understanding romantic relationships, as a result of his own autistic tendencies. He formulated a plan based on three criteria: "I decided that if a woman displayed the three behaviors of hugging, kissing, and initiating handholding, she wanted to be my girlfriend" (p.310). He built in the ability to agree, disagree, or think further about it, as appropriate to the situation and the person. This is an excellent solution and guideline for most people to follow. Either party is responsible for making it known if they're not ready or not interested. In cases where one person does not respect the other's wishes, the latter should understand that his or her needs are not being taken seriously, and that this is not okay. In fact, continuing sexual advances when a person says no can result in a charge of sexual assault (Shore and Rastelli 2006). The utmost important characteristic of any relationship, and most certainly of an intimate, romantic relationship, is respect. *No respect = no relationship!*

LEARN EXPECTATIONS ABOUT MARRIAGE

Although learning about marriage is not specifically relevant to college education or performance, many people do meet their future spouse while in college. Therefore, information about marriage and what it means from a legal, ethical, emotional, and personal perspective should be made available to adults with ASD. It is important for the individual to understand the difference between sexual desires, and feelings of love for a person with whom they want to spend the rest of their lives. Parents should not assume that their child with ASD is learning about marital relationships from themselves as role models. Explicit instruction is required in order to understand the benefits, risks, and requirements of a long-term marital relationship.

LEARN THEORY OF MIND SKILLS

I've referred to the *Theory of Mind* (ToM) concept at times throughout this chapter, and its appearance now at the end of the chapter is intentional. ToM is at the heart of every single interaction we have with other people, and for individuals with ASD it represents a significant area of challenge. It is also one of the most challenging areas to remediate. ToM "is defined as the ability to infer other people's mental states (their thoughts, beliefs, desires, intentions, etc.), and the ability to use this information to interpret what they say, make sense of their behavior and predict what they will do next" (Howlin *et al.* 1999, p.2). These abilities are often well developed in typically developing children as young as four years of age.

While young children are usually able to describe some of their own thought processes and aspects of their own minds, they do not "recognize that they are the authority on knowledge about themselves" until approximately six to seven years of age (Mitchell and O'Keefe 2008, p.1591). In a study comparing levels of "interior self-knowledge" between a sample of 16–50-year-old "non-clinical" individuals and a group of individuals with ASD, Mitchell and O'Keefe (2008) report several interesting findings. Interior self-knowledge is defined as "knowledge about you that another person might not know unless you told them" (p.1591). Subjects were asked to compare and contrast their own level of interior self-knowledge to that of a close "comparison individual" (e.g. an important significant other, parent, etc.). The ASD sample's responses suggest that individuals with ASD did "not recognize themselves as the authority on knowing about themselves, as if they did not appreciate the epistemic value of having first-person privileged access to their own subjective states" (p.1595).

This study (Mitchell and O'Keefe 2008) speaks to the developmental trajectory of self-awareness and the influence of self-awareness on the development of ToM. The understanding that we are the masters of our own minds has multiple implications. First and foremost, it represents the preliminary awareness of a "mind." Without awareness of one's own mind, one will have only limited awareness of another person's mind.

The assumption that others may possess equal or similar amounts of knowledge about us as we ourselves do gives rise to the notion of transparency between minds, a "what you see is what you get" attitude that really doesn't apply to the subtleties and nuances of thought, intent, and nonverbal communication. One who adopts this outlook will surely meet with confusion and interpersonal strife.

Understanding differences between minds also has implications for communication. The nuances of pragmatic communication will flow relatively naturally if one knows that others cannot read one's mind, and vice versa. Clearly this is a broad area for consideration and research. The important factor for the purposes of working with students with ASD is to keep in mind the developmental nature of self- and other-awareness, particularly as it pertains to ToM, and that the first step in this process must be to develop a theory of one's own mind.

Howlin *et al.* (1999) describe a number of developmental abilities that comprise ToM, or "mind-reading," including: perspective-taking, the ability to understand desire, belief, and emotion, and the ability to integrate these areas to understand how someone will feel, based on his or her beliefs, desires, emotions and points of view. This information is used to understand behavior and predict what another person might do. ToM skills also help us understand communicative intent and figurative speech. As noted by Howlin *et al.* (1999), "in decoding speech we are doing a lot more than simply working through the spoken words. We are going beyond what we hear, to hypothesize about the speaker's mental state" (p.6).

The four final uses of mind-reading outlined by Howlin *et al.* include: 1) deception ("making someone believe that something is true when it is actually false"), 2) empathy ("an ability to infer how someone might be interpreting events and how they may be feeling"), 3) self-awareness (the ability to reflect on one's own mind, recognize one's faults and the causes of one's behavior, focus on one's own subjectivity, and "rehearse possible solutions to problems…before actually trying" 4) persuasion ("teaching or attempting to change a person's mind" and recognizing "that other people's thoughts and beliefs are shaped by the information to which they are exposed"). (Howlin *et al.* 1999, p.7).

These authors also recommend providing instruction in three areas:

- Emotions: Understanding others' emotions, including facial expressions and emotions based on situations, desires, and beliefs.

- Informational states: Understanding false beliefs; practice with visual perspective taking and developing an awareness that "seeing leads to knowing"; and learning to predict another person's actions based on what they know.

- Pretend play: Developing all aspects of play, from sensorimotor exploration, to functional play, to symbolic play.

Impairments in ToM result in significant interpersonal anxiety and misunderstanding. Individuals who struggle in this area may be perceived as insensitive to other people's feelings and as misinterpreting others' intentions, which often makes them appear disrespectful and rude. They can be seen as black-and-white or literal thinkers who struggle when things aren't specific, or who respond in unusual ways to metaphor or sarcasm. The idea that others might be devious or deceptive is often difficult for them to comprehend, and as already mentioned, individuals with ASD can become targets of predators, or victims of all kinds of maltreatment. Helping individuals dissect and understand the various aspects of ToM through role-playing, Social Stories™, and some of the newer computer and virtual reality games being developed, will enable them to navigate through these situations more smoothly. Finally, ToM skills evolve in a developmental fashion and need to be stimulated in developmentally appropriate ways throughout the individual's life. For example, the perspective-taking skills of a three-year-old are quite different from those of an adolescent and an adult. Progressive learning that builds on previously attained skills is the most likely formula for success.

PART III
Going to College

Chapter 9

THE BIG DECISION: TO GO OR NOT TO GO?

I recommend middle school as the stage when students and their families begin addressing the possibility of going to college. If a student wants to go to college, a good transition plan needs to be developed in high school. However, by now I hope to have convinced you that there are a number of information processing and independent living skills that need to be developed way before the high-school years! A solid high-school transition plan is essential and should address the necessary skills a particular student will need to develop in order to be successful in college, and beyond. Transition plans will be discussed later in this chapter. For now, let's look at the process of determining whether or not to pursue a post-secondary education (PSE).

IS IT THE RIGHT CHOICE?

In the process of developing readiness skills, students need to consider the various issues related to pursuing a college education. The first issue is whether college is the right choice for that particular student. Although this may be a controversial statement in our current society, not everyone needs to go to college in order to attain their specific career goals—there are many ways to achieve different goals, and college isn't the answer for everything or everyone. Vocational schools, adult education, internships, volunteer opportunities, and apprenticeships are also very viable alternatives to college, depending on the student's career/vocational interests.

Although many students begin their college education without specific career goals in mind, it is important to identify a student's interests, skills, and future goals before embarking on the tremendous responsibility, commitment, and stress inherent in pursuing a college education. For students with ASD, this is particularly important because of the many issues discussed in the previous chapters.

Careful consideration must be given to the student's desire to attend college, but also to the student's readiness, career goals, requirements of the particular career of interest, appropriate fit of the desired career choice for the student, and the various means of attaining the education, training, and skills for that career. Some careers may favor the more practical, hands-on approach commonly found in apprenticeship or internship models, where working with a mentor is seen as more valuable than "book learning." Internships can be very useful for students who aren't sure what they want to do. Another excellent approach to exploring potential jobs or careers is to find business people who are willing to allow the student to shadow or spend time with them on the job (Coulter 2008).

It is crucial to help students develop greater awareness of their strengths and weaknesses, interests, cognitive abilities, and skills in an effort to guide them through this very important decision-making process. This is where a good evaluation can be very useful. I recommend that students undergo a complete neuropsychological evaluation by a private practitioner in their sophomore or junior year of high school. In addition to a general battery of psychological tests, the neuropsychological evaluation includes a number of other tests that provide information about the student's learning style, specific brain-based challenges, and how they will impact the student's learning and education. The evaluation should also recommend appropriate accommodations for the college setting. This type of evaluation serves many purposes. It clarifies the student's strengths and weaknesses and identifies various compensatory strategies that will help the student maximize his learning and enhance his ability to benefit from his education. It also provides the documentation required by most colleges when students need accommodations in that setting. Although a neuropsychological evaluation can be costly, the findings can clarify many issues and make a valuable contribution to the student's current and future education.

A vocational or career assessment can also be beneficial, especially if the student does not know what direction he wants to take after high school. The career office at the student's high school might have access to this type of evaluation, or can refer the family to a private practitioner. If a student is eligible, the state Department of Vocational Rehabilitation (DOR) can also provide this service, but probably not until the student graduates from high school. Most students who receive special education services in high school have an Individualized Education Plan (IEP), and transition services through the DOR may be available to them. Parents are encouraged to ask about this and request that the transition process include a meeting with a case manager from the state's DOR. (Please note that these government agencies may have different names in different states.) The DOR helps adults with disabilities map out the course of study or training needed to find successful vocations, careers, and employment. There may be financial assistance for students who become eligible for these services. Each state has its own regulations and funding issues. I recommend that parents contact the nearest DOR office and obtain information about eligibility and available services.

Regardless of assessment findings, any student who truly wants to go to college needs to be encouraged and supported in their decision. Education and career goals need to be identified and the viability of the student's career interests determined, taking into consideration the student's overall cognitive, physical, social, and emotional profile. For example, I worked with an individual who enjoyed lifting weights and knew a great deal about the legal system. He wanted to pursue training as a police officer because he was very interested in upholding the law and fighting crime on the streets. However, his ability to make rapid assessments about a person's intentions was significantly impaired, as was his ability to read nonverbal cues. Therefore this was a poor career choice, not only in terms of his own safety, but also for the safety of the community and his fellow workers.

Career and vocational testing can be very useful in cases where students' aspirations may not suit their overall profile, or when students are unclear as to which direction they want to take. It also takes the onus off parents when a student's aspirations are inconsistent with his abilities. Students can suffer disappointment as a result of this process. They may have developed a rather rigid fixation on pursuing a particular career, and to find out that they are not suited for it can be devastating. Often they have limited awareness of their own strengths and weaknesses, especially in the interpersonal realm, and possibly also limited awareness of the specific requirements of their career choice. Working with a career counselor or mental health practitioner with expertise in ASD can be instrumental in helping students to work through these feelings and move forward in a different direction, if necessary.

If a student is hesitant about college, then it is important to identify why. The student's reasoning may be based on a general lack of interest in pursuing a college education, in which case her wish needs to be respected and alternative plans developed. If a student is concerned about her ability to succeed in college, it may be possible for her to take a class at a local college just to see what it's like. This can often take place while the student is still in high school during the school year, or in the summer.

Many students reject the idea of college because it's an unknown and a huge transition for them. However, fear is not a valid reason to avoid something. I consider this an issue that is best addressed by a mental health professional to help the student understand her fear and find a way of preventing it from overwhelming her decision-making powers.

I work with many bright students who, after an extremely negative high-school experience, want no more schooling after graduation. Some students erroneously think that college will be just like high school. Educating them about college life and encouraging them (with assistance) to talk to professors and other college students about their specific concerns will enable them to make a more informed decision. Other students may simply want a break from schooling. For them, finding a job or pursuing training in an area of interest may be the right choice. If at a later stage they feel prepared to pursue a college education, they can do so.

There is no law that says students have to begin college immediately after graduating from high school. In fact, many students may not be ready, or might benefit from having a different, less academic experience. The most important thing that students need to know is that the door to higher education is always open, no matter what decision they make immediately after high school. It can be helpful for students to understand that everyone's life takes its own individual path. Some people go to college right after high school and continue straight through until they've achieved whatever level of education they desire. However, even those people may return to college at any time later in their lives. Others may decide against college at first, and then later change their minds. Others may choose a completely different path that does not include college. All of these decisions and choices are acceptable, and there is no one right choice for everyone. Once we become adults, we are the architects and designers of our destiny and we can construct our lives in any way that feels appropriate at different junctures.

Many colleges encourage students to take a year off between high school and college. This is called the "gap year." Colleges value the experience of working in the community, developing a greater sense of maturity prior to beginning a college education, and recovering from the rigors of high school and the college application process (Newmarker 2008). There are numerous national and international community service programs designed to take place during the gap year. It also offers students an opportunity to participate in part-time employment, volunteer or internship positions in their areas of interest. By participating in these types of experiences students may be better able to hone in more precisely on their abilities, interests, and future course of study. These opportunities can also help students become more familiar with the types of employment opportunities available in their particular areas of interest.

Students may be more inclined to participate in a gap year program when they know they have a secured college place and that they won't have to re-apply after the gap year is over. However, some students will absolutely refuse to take a break between high school and college because they want to follow in their peers' footsteps. These are all issues that can be addressed with a therapist and/or a college counselor so that students make a decision that is right for them.

Finally, a number of interim summer camps for high-school students and more extensive structured transition programs for high-school graduates are available. These programs are designed to prepare high-school students and graduates for a college experience. Students who are anxious about going to college or leaving home may benefit from participating in these more supportive programs. Enrolling students in this type of program is an excellent way of addressing students' anxiety about going to college or leaving home by showing them that they can, in fact, be successful on their own. These programs are also very useful for students who need additional support in independent living skills and executive functioning. A good neuropsychological evaluation can help determine whether a student would benefit from participating in a more structured, supportive kind of program.

YES, IT'S THE RIGHT CHOICE

Once the decision to go to college is made, a number of other options will need to be considered.

Am I ready to leave home?

In planning for college, the student and other adults in their support system (e.g. parents, therapists, counselors, case coordinators) need to consider whether the student is ready to go away for college, would be better off spending one or two years at home at a local community college, or would be better served by attending a transitional readiness or more structured college program first. Students need to understand that any of these options are perfectly acceptable, and that the one to select is the one that will most quickly and successfully enable the student to accomplish his or her future goals.

Often students feel as if they have failed if they can't immediately leave home to attend a four-year college course like many of their typically developing peers do. This is a natural reaction and often occurs as a result of students' ongoing awareness that they are "different." Students who cannot get past these feelings are probably struggling with self-acceptance. Working with a counselor or therapist can help them develop greater self-awareness and self-acceptance.

Some students may have a misconception about making this decision. For example, Nick Dubin (2005) decided to go away for college because he thought that it was "un-cool" to stay home. Unfortunately, leaving home was the wrong decision for Nick, but no one questioned it. Nick, and other students like him, will benefit from having someone neutral to talk with about their perceptions, so that they can make a decision based on their own needs, not on how others will judge them or on the choices that others make for themselves.

Leaving home for college can feel very abrupt for some students (Perner 2007). The many transitions and unknowns of higher education can cause high levels of anxiety in many students, and this is especially true for students with ASD. Most students who do go away for college arrive at their school approximately one week before classes start. In that week they set up their room, register for classes, and figure out where their classes are. This is the time when students meet and adjust to their roommate(s), and participate in dorm parties and other unpredictable activities. For some this can be very challenging, and others may actually need more time to adjust.

Some people believe that leaving home forces students to mature, while staying home can hamper maturity because students are not "forced" to fend for themselves. While many students who struggle socially report that being away from their families increases their loneliness and feelings of depression, others note that their social lives improve as a result of being away from home. This important decision needs to be balanced and individualized to meet the particular student's profile of strengths and weaknesses.

My hope is that as we become better able to prepare students to function independently away from home, more students who would like to go away for college will feel comfortable doing so. Finding the right school and an appropriate, caring Disabilities Services Advisor can make a big difference in a student's willingness to leave home. Students are more likely to succeed when they receive the appropriate supports and tools in the college environment. Parents can be instrumental in making sure that the Disabilities Services Advisor understands the student and is willing to utilize within the college setting the tools and types of supports that were helpful and facilitated success in high school. These assurances can help students explore all of their options and enable them to make an informed decision about whether to leave or stay home.

Am I ready to live in close quarters with a roommate, do I want a roommate with ASD, or do I need to request a single room?

These are very important questions that should be considered prior to applying to a college, because many colleges simply do not offer single rooms to freshmen. For those that do, there may be restrictions and deadlines that need to be met and additional costs that need to be considered.

There are many factors involved in determining whether a student can manage living with a roommate. Dorm rooms tend to be very small and can feel claustrophobic once two people have all of their belongings in place. Dorm living requires that roommates be sensitive to one another in terms of neatness, noise, sharing responsibilities, being considerate when having friends over, etc. This level of sensitivity is required of both roommates, and there are no guarantees that either one will fulfill their obligation. Dorm living requires respecting personal space and asking permission before touching a roommate's belongings. For students who struggle with sensory overload, dorm living can be difficult and overwhelming, especially for those who thrive on maintaining their routines and struggle with unpredictability. All of these factors must be considered when making a decision about where the student will live.

Dorm living can be stressful for *any* student, and many students, both with and without ASD, may need help interfacing and getting along with their roommates. I strongly recommend disclosure of one's disability to the resident advisor (RA). A caring and available RA can help iron out problems and make dorm living fun. Most RAs receive training in conflict resolution and problem-solving. It is to be hoped that in the not-so-distant future they will also receive specific training in helping students with ASD have a positive dorm and roommate experience. Although it may be possible to request a roommate who also has ASD, there are no guarantees, primarily because disclosure is not mandatory.

What kind of school is right for me?

In order to determine this, I recommend working with a college placement consultant who understands ASD and can direct students to the most appropriate schools. There are many factors to consider, and students may find themselves having to choose between the school of their "dreams," and the school that will most effectively meet their needs and enable them to have a positive and successful college experience. Students may resist certain options (e.g. vocational school) because they have a strong desire to follow the same path as many of their typically developing peers.

Overall, universities and colleges typically adopt one of three different philosophies about students with disabilities. The first results in the provision of a basic level of support, as required by law. This can include basic accommodations, such as extended time for tests, taking tests in a distraction-free location, using anonymous note-takers, etc. Generally speaking, colleges falling into this category are probably not a good choice for most students with ASD. The second philosophical perspective results in the provision of more coordinated support services, which include basic accommodations as well as additional levels of support (e.g. peer tutoring, hands-on assistance from a Disabilities Services Advisor on a regular basis, referral to other services available in the community), usually for a fee. The third philosophical viewpoint is more comprehensive, offering a more supportive model that can include all of the above, plus specific tutoring (e.g. in time management and organization skills), social skills groups, mentoring or coaching (peer or professional), and ASD-specific counseling or psychotherapy. These can be included in the overall tuition, or fee-based. Students with ASD are more likely to succeed in programs that offer coordinated and comprehensive support services.

Junior College

Most cities across the country have "JCs" that are excellent options for some students. Most students attend JCs for a variety of reasons, but the most common reason is that JCs cost significantly less than four-year colleges, and at a JC students can complete the first two years of basic core courses required at a four-year college at a significantly lower cost. Some students who may not feel ready to leave home or enter into the world of a four-year college may feel more comfortable starting their education at a local JC. Completion of a two-year course of study at a JC usually results in attaining an associate's degree.

Before making a decision to go to a JC, there are a few things to consider. What is its ability to meet the specific needs of students with disabilities? If a student needs a fair amount of support, a JC may not be an appropriate choice. JCs are typically commuter schools where students go to campus primarily for classes, and then leave. Therefore, social life can be limited at a JC and some students do feel isolated as a result. Even if there are social activities at the JC, students have to seek them out more purposefully than at a four-year college, where announcements about social events are typically posted in dorms and other gathering places on campus.

While staying home may be appealing for many students with ASD, it can also delay the student's maturation process. When working with a student to help her decide between a JC and a four-year college, it's important to look at the student's needs and the reason(s) why she prefers one over the other. If her primary reason for selecting a JC is fear, we work towards limiting the "control" that fear exerts on her, so that a more objective decision process can take place.

Another factor to consider is whether a student would be better off at a JC than at a four-year college. Independence is a very important skill. The student's level of independence, and her family's capacity for fostering independence in her, can both be determining factors. If both factors are low, I strongly urge students to attend a supportive transitional program because it may be the only way for them to develop independent living skills.

When considering the possibility of attending a JC, the pros and cons of transferring to another school for the junior and senior year must also be considered. Transferring schools can be difficult for any student. Students who attend a JC will complete their first two years of a four-year college there. Assimilating into a program where everyone else is already comfortable and situated can also be very challenging. Finding one's social group in this type of setting can be difficult, because by their junior year most students have already selected their group of friends. This scenario will be fraught with even more challenges for the student with ASD who already experiences multiple socially related struggles.

Large universities

Many students dream of going to a large university. In the area where I practice, the University of California Los Angeles (UCLA) is a highly desired school for many high-school students, and I have met a small group of students who have successfully navigated their education there with the support of Disabilities Services.

A large university can have many benefits and drawbacks. Some of the benefits include: a large pool of students to draw from for social contact; numerous campus clubs and activities to meet the needs of many different types of students; attending a highly recognized and respected school (although in the long run this may be less important than most think); strong athletic programs; and the university may be relatively close to home for easier access to parents and family. I strongly urge students who decide to attend a large university to live on campus, in order to benefit from the full university experience.

The drawbacks to a large university setting for students with ASD can include the following. Large classrooms (100–400 students) do not lend themselves to individualization and result in less contact with professors, who cannot know or have a feel for each student in their classes; and large classes present more distractions and risk of sensory overload. Long absences would probably not be noticed by a professor, unless a student missed a test. Exams at large universities are corrected electronically, and professors rarely connect test grades with particular students. In a large classroom the professor might not notice unusual behaviors, but other students sitting nearby would. This could result in the student with ASD being mocked or avoided by peers. In addition to large classes, a sizable university setting can feel overwhelming, especially for students who have trouble navigating large geographical settings. Classes can be spread out over the campus, making it difficult to arrive to class on time. Finally, while some may think that students can receive more specialized support at a larger university, this is not always true, and depends on the particular university's philosophies and practices. Access to a student's Disabilities Services Advisor may (although not necessarily) be more difficult at a larger school due to higher numbers of students on an advisor's caseload. On the other hand, some larger universities are likely to have more funding available to develop their Disabilities Services department, and may have more resources to offer.

The best way to make a decision about which PSE institution suits a particular student is to identify the student's needs, strengths, and weaknesses, work and life goals, and any other pertinent factors. The right school is one that will meet the student's learning and social–emotional needs, while affording the student the most promising opportunity for success. Fortunately there are so many colleges and universities to consider, that finding a good match should be relatively easy. Some key questions to ask are:

- What type of training do Disabilities Services staff get on ASD?

- How are professors, resident advisors, and public safety personnel trained on working with students with ASD?

- What types of accommodations are available, and are they willing to provide the kind of accommodations that the student needs?

- Does the college offer any structured or unstructured opportunities for developing and improving socialization skills?

- Is it possible to arrange for a peer or professional mentor?

- Are there any autism-related organizations for students on campus?

Smaller universities

The right small college can offer many advantages to students with disabilities. At most small schools class sizes are small (20–50), and personal contact with professors is often relatively easy. Small class sizes lend themselves to more personal contact and assistance between student and professor, and student concerns can be dealt with more readily. Professors at smaller schools have more time to provide students with feedback about their work, and personal contact leads to familiarity, making it more likely that a student with ASD will approach a professor. Sensory issues are reduced when the number of students in a room is smaller, and managing a smaller campus can significantly reduce a student's anxiety and navigational challenges. Dorms can be smaller, and again, more personal relationships can be established with RAs. Access to one's advisor and other necessary administrative staff can also feel more manageable for the student. Although there may be fewer students to choose from, most people attending small schools do make friends and find their social niche.

Online learning

While this form of learning has not been widely utilized until recently, there is a strong push for online learning, and it is appealing to students for whom the demands of participation in classrooms and college campuses are less desirable and more challenging. Many universities also encourage online learning because it provides a higher return on their investment than traditional classroom teaching. While universities must meet the initial cost of developing the electronic educational package, this is often a one-time expense, although there are also costs associated with maintenance of the hosting site, and some administrative costs. However, compared to the costs of employing professors, providing classroom settings, and maintaining classrooms and buildings that house them, etc., the costs of online learning are likely to be significantly lower.

Although online learning affords students the opportunity for higher education, it does not offer opportunities for increasing and improving interpersonal skills. Most students who enter the workforce will need some level of proficiency in interpersonal skills to interface with bosses, colleagues, and customers or clients. Students with ASD typically develop their interpersonal abilities as they mature and become young adults, and by choosing online learning, they may be depriving themselves of an opportunity to develop these skills. Students may not have access to individualized support in an online learning environment. Finally, online learning may not be available or suitable for some courses of study. Therefore these factors should be carefully considered before selecting this model of education. I recommend that students attempt at least one semester and preferably one year in a college setting prior to committing to online learning, or perhaps the student can combine online learning with taking one or two classes at a university or college in order to experience both and make a more informed decision about which is more appropriate.

Many students that I work with are terrified about the unknowns of going to college. Their fears can overwhelm and overcome their ability to make objective decisions. Clinicians play an important role in helping students recognize and manage any fears that interfere in their ability to make this very important decision.

Other options

As mentioned above, college may not be the right or necessary choice for every student. Depending on the student's career or job interests, a vocational or trade school, a technical institute, or a certificate program may be the best choice.

Personalized college tour and instructions for getting started

Touring the campus prior to beginning classes is common practice. Although most colleges do not offer individual or small group orientations for students with disabilities, some schools will honor requests for a personalized tour once the student is accepted and has committed to the college. Because Disabilities Services Offices (DSO) and other personnel are inundated during the beginning of the school year, flexibility in scheduling a personalized tour, or any other individualized assistance, will be essential. In many cases these requests can be honored on an individual basis at a time that is convenient to both the student and the DSO.

The ins and outs of course selection

The entire process of selecting appropriate courses, planning for courses that are only offered during one specific semester and prerequisite courses, learning the rules and deadlines for adding or dropping classes, etc., can be overwhelming for any student. Students with ASD need to work closely with their DSO advisor when planning and selecting specific courses. A good DSO advisor can recommend professors who have been open to working with students with disabilities in the past, and can help streamline the registration process. The overall flexibility and inherent control that students have in selecting courses can be appealing to students with ASD, as long as they understand the process and can see the "big picture." Using visual cues, such as mapping out an entire academic year or two at a time, can help with this. Students will need to adapt to scheduling conflicts that arise as a result of specific classes being offered only at specific times. However, most students are able to work through these occasional roadblocks. Finally, careful attention needs to be paid to the timing of the student's classes, allowing as much time as possible between classes so as to avoid excessive anxiety about getting to class on time.

Course selection can make a big difference in a student's adjustment to college. An extremely important aspect of this for the student with ASD is to ensure a balance between courses that fall into the student's preferred areas of interest and those that are non-preferred. A schedule of exclusively non-preferred classes is a recipe for disaster! Although most students complete basic core courses during their first two years of college, this may not be a useful path for the student with ASD, who is more likely to succeed if she is encouraged to combine less preferred classes with more enjoyable classes, rather than follow a prescribed course of study. Students who would benefit from adopting this approach to course selection should make sure that the college they choose is amenable to it. There will be students who resist this idea, especially if it means delaying graduation and/or not graduating at the same time as their peers. It may take a little time and effort to work through this, but the bottom line is that it's better to graduate than to drop out.

The student–advisor relationship

I highly recommend that all students with disabilities be required to meet weekly with their DSO advisor, especially for the student's first year at school. This can be the single most important relationship in a student's PSE, and a good advisor will try to do whatever it takes to ensure the student's success.

Asking for a mentor, therapist, tutor or coach to help with personal issues

Many innovative programs are being developed for students with ASD, and the use of mentors and coaches is inherent in those programs. A mentor could be another student whose area of study is related to understanding people with differences—psychology, speech and language pathology, sociology, or special education, for instance. If coaches or mentors are unavailable at a particular college but all of the other pieces fall into place, parents can consider hiring a student to fulfill the role of mentor (Adreon and Durocher 2007). Parents may want to consider offering the student in this role some training with a local expert in ASD, or at an upcoming conference.

Adjusting to college life is stressful for all students, and those with ASD may need more "down" time than most other students during this adjustment period. They will also need to learn a number of new "social conventions" for appropriate behavior in numerous new settings (Attwood 2007). Many students with ASD report feelings of loneliness but don't know what to do about them. They want to get involved in social events or clubs sponsored by the school, but they may not have the skills to do so and would benefit from assistance. Involvement in extracurricular activities and school clubs can be an important avenue to develop important contacts for when the student is ready for employment.

Teaching students that feelings of loneliness are important and necessitate asking for help will go a long way toward preventing withdrawal. This is important because loneliness and isolation are the most common contributors to suicidal ideation in college students. Some students report spending their free time at the library, "where it's quiet and social skills are rarely necessary" (Pantak 2007). A mentor or coach can be instrumental in identifying students who spend too much time at the library, and helping them become more comfortable on campus.

A mentor or coach can also provide a number of other supports, with the primary purpose being to minimize as much as possible the student's stress level over basic stumbling blocks. Some of these stumbling blocks can include using one's campus ID and/or charge card; getting around campus or using maps to find classes; finding restrooms in various areas on campus; the ins and outs of campus mail; how and when to access student health services; what to do when first aid is necessary; what to do if the student gets sick; how to deal with meal plans; cafeteria rules and times; where to eat if not in the cafeteria; what to do when an ID, ATM or credit card is lost. Clearly, having regular contact with someone on campus can be crucial for students with learning differences and social–emotional challenges.

Consider disclosure to other students in one's classes

Over the years, I have encouraged my clients to talk about their challenges with their peers and with their teachers. "Knowledge is power," and the more knowledge their peers and teachers have about the student, the more educated and comfortable they will feel interacting with him or her.

Students who have been willing to disclose their challenges have told me that it was the best thing they ever did, and continually thank me for guiding them through the process. There are many options for how disclosure can happen. Some students opt to write a script with me and their parent(s), which we film as a video that is viewed in class, followed by questions and answers that the student (and parent, as appropriate) participate(s) in. Some high-school students opt to disclose only to specific peers or in specific classes (e.g. the class in which they feel least confident or get teased in). None of the students who have disclosed has ever experienced a negative outcome as a result of doing so. Beginning this process before the student moves on to PSE will go a long way towards helping him feel more comfortable disclosing in the college setting.

TRANSITION PLANNING

Transition planning is defined in the USA under the Individuals with Disabilities Education Act (IDEA) as a means by which, while the student is still in high school (and possibly earlier), to prepare her for her future endeavors. In my opinion, it is the cornerstone of how we think about developing the necessary core skills for success in life *before* students leave high school.

The key to successful transition planning for parents and professionals is familiarity with all of the available federal laws and programs that provide for the protection and support of individuals with disabilities. Familiarity breeds access—the more familiar professionals and parents become with these laws and programs, the more likely the student is to have access to them. VanBergeijk *et al.* (2008) suggest that the transition plan "include exposure to the college curriculum while the student is still in high school" (p.1363). The authors support models currently being used in New York, where students participate in a "Grade 13" by attending college level courses "at the local community college in the morning" and "return to their high schools for academic and social support" in the afternoon (p.1363). Creative school districts will be at the forefront of developing standards that will enable students with ASD to maximize their potential and meet with success in whatever PSE option they select. What will subsequently be needed is a creative plan to support individuals in transition from PSE or vocational training to the workplace. After years of acclimating to college life, this transition can be extremely stressful for students with ASD who are at risk for developing "an acute psychiatric crisis in response to the stress of the pending transition to post college life" (VanBergeijk *et al.* 2008, p.1368).

The programs and laws described below include: Individuals with Disabilities Education Act (IDEA), Section 504 of the Vocational Rehabilitation Act of 1973, the Americans with Disabilities Amendments Act (ADA), Social Security Administration, and the Federal Education Rights and Privacy Act (FERPA).

Individuals with Disabilities Education Act (IDEA)

IDEA is the federal law that governs the primary and secondary education of students. IDEA states that all students are entitled to a free and appropriate public education (FAPE) in the least restrictive environment (LRE). A 2004 modification to IDEA specifically addresses the school district's obligation to ensure that students are prepared for their future endeavors, whether it be PSE, vocational training, supported or integrated employment, and community integration/independent living (Gerhardt 2009a). In order to accomplish this, the development of a transitional IEP is required to take place no later than the student's sixteenth birthday, but can happen anytime before that, as deemed appropriate. IDEA states that discussion of transition services needs to begin, one way or another, by the student's fourteenth birthday. I strongly recommend that parents ask for a transitional IEP as early as possible and appropriate, because students with ASD will likely require more intensive and longer intervention to build "strengths-based skills."

The transition planning requirements of IDEA focus on developing the student's existing abilities, not on improving areas of deficit.

Although working on skill deficits can continue to be a part of the student's regular IEP, it is implied that by the time a transitional IEP occurs, the student's areas of deficits will predominantly be improved. While this may not be true in many cases, it is a worthy aspiration. However, because the average age of diagnosis continues to be seven to ten years of age, most intervention for students with ASD does not begin until their mid-elementary school years, and so many students continue to need intervention for skill development well into their high-school years.

While its intentions are good, the concept of transition planning is, at best, inconsistantly successful due to a lack of professional and parental awareness. Transition plans should include academic, self-advocacy, and independent living skills goals, and any other areas of need for each student to succeed in his or her next step beyond high school. Goals can be met both within the high-school setting and in other community-based environments, and it is essential that coordination of services with all current and potential service delivery systems occurs at the time of the transitional IEP. According to Gerhardt (2009a), "Even the best school-based transition programs will be of little benefit if they are not coordinated with the state's adult service system...the best planning cannot overcome the prospect of nothing on the other side of transition" (p.13). I encourage parents to become familiar with the intricacies of the law and the rights and entitlements that it provides to students, especially those related to inter-agency participation and providing appropriate transition services (see the following sections of this chapter for details on other potential agencies that can become involved). I also encourage parents to use a special education advocate to ensure that the goals and level of intervention being recommended are appropriate, and that services are being provided in an appropriate manner and in compliance with the law. Once the transition process is implemented successfully, we should see a significant increase in successful PSE and satisfactory employment of individuals with all types of disabilities.

Students with ASD will need a significantly more intensive transition program than many other students at the same level of cognitive ability (e.g. students with learning disabilities) due to their information processing and executive functioning impairments. They will also benefit from more than a simple, school-to-work transition plan. Therefore, the concept of transition planning for these students necessitates careful consideration and planning, and also "needs to go beyond traditional classroom activities...include opportunities for the acquisition of self-awareness, self-advocacy, and social skills that the young adult will need to live and work in the adult world" (Korpi 2008, p.23). Whenever students are not provided with appropriate transition services, it may be possible for them to receive post-graduation intervention or relief, according to the authors of the online resource "SmartStart: Decisions about Graduation:"

> IDEA-eligible students cannot be graduated until they receive appropriate transition services. Were it otherwise, the school district would violate its duty to provide FAPE with immunity. Students who are graduated without transition services are entitled to post-graduation relief. See *J.B.* v. *Killingly Board of Education*, 27 IDELR 324 (D. Conn. 1995), (awarding compensatory relief when a school district fails to provide appropriate transition services prior to awarding a regular high school diploma). See also *Novato Unified School District*, 22 IDELR 1056 (SEA CA 1995), (awarding additional period of residential placement to a student with an emotional disturbance who had not received community experiences in his local community prior to his graduation).

Department of Developmental Disabilities (DDS)

All states have a state department for individuals with developmental disabilities. In California, the DDS coordinates and oversees the entire provision of services, while local Regional Centers for Individuals with Disabilities (RC) assess and disseminate various services to individuals with disabilities. Eligibility criteria differ from state to state, and in the state of California may also differ from RC to RC. Unfortunately, funding issues play a large role in the availability of services as well as in eligibility standards. All students with ASD should apply for eligibility to their local RC/DDS. There are built-in appeal procedures that enable parents to appeal a decision to deny services, and often parents prevail at these appeals. Even if a student was denied services as a child, I encourage clients to re-apply, either when they graduate from middle school, just before their eighteenth birthday, or at any time during their adult lives, because there are numerous services that apply to older individuals with disabilities. Based on individual need, RCs can fund social skills programs, independent living skills training, behavior therapy, job mentoring, and other services. If an individual is a client of the local RC, his or her case manager should be invited to the transition planning IEP meeting.

In summary, smooth interface between school districts and other federally and state-funded agencies and programs is very important. According to Pratt (2007), "Agencies must work with schools to identify students early, begin to actively work with the school team to get to know the student, and begin to identify adult services and potential employment. Timelines vary from state to state and agency to agency. Funding and eligibility requirements may get in the way of a smooth transition. In fact, funding will always be an issue. However, agencies must begin to create opportunities to work together systematically so that the transition is seamless, or at least does not unravel altogether" (p.9).

RESOURCES FOR LIFE AFTER HIGH SCHOOL

Once students reach the age of 18, there are other legal protections and services that are available to facilitate their integration and access to basic community activities and employment, whether or not they decide to embark on PSE.

Department of Vocational Rehabilitation (DOR)

The Vocational Rehabilitation Act of 1973 (VRA) was designed to enable individuals with disabilities to have access to programs receiving federal funds, and to provide job training. Amendments to VRA were developed in an effort to employ *all* individuals with disabilities, regardless of the severity of disability (Gerhardt 2009a). A representative from the DOR should be invited to the student's transition planning IEP meeting.

The actual efficacy and implementation of these programs varies across states, and funding issues often interfere. According to Johnson (2007), the following services are paid for and provided by DOR:

> Assessments to determine eligibility and needs; counseling, guidance and job-placement services; training, and purchase of tools, materials

and books; maintenance for costs incurred during rehabilitation; diagnosis and treatment of physical or mental impairment to reduce or eliminate impediments to employment when comparable benefits are not available. These may include: corrective surgery; therapeutic treatment; prosthetic and orthotic devices; eyeglasses and visual services; diagnosis and treatment for mental or emotional disorders. Transportation: including training, vehicle modification and purchase; personal assistance while receiving VR [vocational rehabilitation] services; interpreter services, readers, rehab teaching; occupational licenses, tools, equipment, initial stocks and supplies; technical assistance for self-employment; rehab technology; transition services for students with disabilities; supported employment help; services to family to help persons with disability achieve employment outcome; post-employment services necessary to assist an individual to retain, regain or advance in employment. (pp.11–12)

Section 504 of the Vocational Rehabilitation Act

This is the portion of the law that entitles individuals with disabilities to equal and appropriate access to organizations and employers who receive federal financial support. Any universities that receive direct federal financial support (i.e. grants), or accept federally sponsored student loans, are obligated to meet the minimum requirements of Section 504.

The Americans with Disabilities Act (ADA)

The ADA entitles individuals with qualified disabilities to equal access to public activities, organizations, or employers, regardless of whether federal funds are involved. It prohibits discrimination against individuals with disabilities and ensures that individuals will receive appropriate accommodations to ensure access within these various environments. In the workplace, ADA specifies the provision of "reasonable accommodations" to able workers so that they can perform the essential functions of a job. Accommodations are intended to level the playing field between individuals who are disabled and those who are not. According to Gerhardt (2009a), "This ruling supports the right of individuals with disabilities to live, work, and enjoy life in the community" (pp.11–12).

Social Security Administration (SSA) benefits

Many individuals with disabilities who are not fully employed may be eligible for SSA benefits, including Social Security Income (SSI), Social Security Disability Income (SSDI), and Medi-Cal/Medicare insurance programs. Eligibility and award criteria vary by state. Once a student reaches the age of 18, his or her parents' income no longer needs to be considered, making it easier to attain eligibility, since income level is a primary determining factor. While in college, this kind of support can be valuable for students with disabilities, who may find it difficult to work part-time but still need financial support for clothing, transportation, and food. Some students may also be eligible for state medical insurance programs, possibly in combination with their own private insurance. In California, Medi-Cal has a "third party billing" program that pays for many medical expenses that are not covered by one's individual or group health insurance plan, provided that a Medi-Cal doctor or pharmacy is used. Students and their parents should check with their local Social Security office to apply for benefits (see Appendix B for contact information).

There are also specific guidelines for eligibility. For example, individuals are not eligible to receive SSA benefits if they have more than $2,000.00 in any kind of savings or checking account, or in a trust that is not protected. (Parents are wise to establish a special needs trust when the student is still a minor.) There are also limitations on how much a full-time college student can earn. While it can be a time-consuming process to familiarize oneself with the guidelines, it is well worth the effort in the long run. Working with knowledgeable professionals can help parents and students understand and access the appropriate services throughout the student's elementary, secondary, and post-secondary years.

Family Educational Rights and Privacy Act (FERPA)

FERPA addresses issues of confidentiality for students attending college. The Family Educational Rights and Privacy Act (FERPA) has strict guidelines for the type of information the DSO can share about students with other PSE staff and with the student's parents. In fact, most colleges will not contact parents unless they absolutely have to. College staff can contact a student's parents only with the student's specific written permission. The DSO will typically use a consent form that enables students to indicate what type of information can be shared. In general, disability and academic information is kept private from anyone other than faculty or other staff who have a true need to know (Johnson and Hines 2005).

I recommend that students and their families become familiar with both the ADA and FERPA guidelines. The respective websites are listed in Appendix B. Another decision that may need to be considered is whether the student needs (and wants) to grant conservatorship (power of attorney) to his parents, even if only for specific concerns (e.g. for making important medical decisions and/or during medical emergencies). Students who struggle to manage their finances will need some type of parental support in this area, although the need for conservatorship, as such, may not be warranted.

Chapter 10

COLLEGES AND PROFESSORS HELPING STUDENTS WITH ASD

If students with autistic spectrum disorders (ASD) are to be successful on college campuses, then college professors, advisors, and others in the role of tutoring or mentoring students with ASD must have at minimum some training on ASD, with awareness of the following:

- The cognitive and learning differences exhibited by this population and the kinds of accommodations that typically benefit learners with these differences. For example, students with ASD tend to be visual learners who typically have some degree of impairment in auditory processing. Visual aids will enhance comprehension of auditory material. Because auditory processing is slow, their response time can also be slow. Therefore, it may be necessary to wait for the student to organize his thoughts before he is able to answer questions.

- Communication challenges and how these challenges may interfere in self-advocacy.

- Strategies to ensure that students understand assignments; recommendation for regular meetings with students if needed.

- The barriers that sensory overload poses to learning in the classroom.

- Time management challenges and the type of assistance necessary to help the student successfully complete assignments.

- Mental health problems that may occur, and their manifestations.

- The importance of fostering personal independence and social adaptation on campus, including friendships, romantic relationships, and relationships with faculty members, so that the student feels accepted and successful.

- Challenges in the area of Theory of Mind (ToM). This is particularly important because ToM challenges can often result in students appearing to be uninterested, rude, or self-absorbed when they do not use the kinds of social courtesies we come to expect in interactions.

Providing staff training up front can mitigate some of the stress students will feel as a result of challenges in these areas. Coulter (2003) suggests offering a file of teaching tips for all disabilities, including ASD, to professors, and also recommends offering training to residential advisors (RAs), particularly in the area of managing potential problems. Evans (2008) notes that "Professors at Marshall [University] are given a profile of each student in their class with Asperger's syndrome. The profile outlines each student's abilities and areas in which they need assistance" (p.1). Helping professors recognize the student's learning style can make a big difference in their ability to understand the student. It is also a useful teaching tool for learning about ASD.

Finally, students with ASD tend to be targets of bullying and victimization more often than students without disabilities, so it is important to train campus security to recognize potential areas of concern, including bullying, potential for stalking, dealing with outbursts, and safety concerns revolving around victimization and/or general lack of awareness (Wolf, Thierfeld Brown and Kukiela Bork 2009).

To this end, it may also be helpful to offer evidence-based safety training instruction to students with ASD geared specifically towards the college environment they will be in. The Autism Society of America has developed first responder training programs, and colleges may want to explore the benefit of disseminating them to campus and local security officers. Useful information can be found on the Autism Risk and Safety Management website developed by Dennis Debbaudt (www. autismriskmanagement.com), where safety issues such as "self-care, sexuality, internet safety, emergency preparedness, and environmental safety at home and in the community" are identified (Gerhardt 2009a).

ACCOMMODATIONS

As mentioned above, universities and colleges who accept any type of federal assistance are obligated to provide equal access for students with disabilities to all campus related services, facilities, and activities. Confidentiality is also guaranteed, as specified by the Family Educational Rights and Privacy Act (FERPA; see pp.189–190). Federal laws also specify that students with disabilities should receive *reasonable* accommodations, auxiliary aids and services, and/or academic adjustments, and written rules and regulations that include grievance procedures.

Accommodations are adjustments or adaptations to an academic program that enable a student with disabilities to participate in it. They also help moderate the impact of the disability on the student's ability to participate effectively. The goal of accommodations is to "level the playing field," not to give students with disabilities an unfair advantage over those without them. What cannot be compromised are academic standards or the fundamental requirements of a particular course of study.

When the concept of accommodations was born, the primary population whose needs were taken into consideration were individuals with physical disabilities (who needed, for example, ramps for wheelchairs, books in Braille, etc.). However, students with ASD and other types of "invisible" disabilities require other kinds of accommodations—some geared towards their individual learning and information processing styles and limitations, others towards their social–emotional processing limitations. The types of accommodations that will level the playing field for students with ASD may be very different from the standard accommodations typically provided by institutions of higher learning, and it is in this area that most colleges will need to develop.

While there are many standard accommodations with which most colleges are familiar, accommodations that focus on helping students with ASD to navigate the social world are not among them. According to Moore (2006), "One disability specialist in Minnesota says interventions to provide social skills training at college is the least they can offer... 'We would provide an interpreter to a hard-of-hearing person. Why don't we provide an interpreter [of social situations] for somebody with Asperger's?'" (p.37). Mentors, tutors, and coaches can be integral in facilitating improved social assimilation for students with ASD.

An accommodation that enables students to check that they have understood all test and assignment questions will help those who are over-literal to avoid failure by misinterpretation. Lars Perner (2007), in his article on preparing for college, discusses his tendency to be over-literal when interpreting test questions. Toward this end, students can be encouraged to check with professors to ensure that they have understood assignment instructions. Some students get confused when instructions are given orally, or when teachers announce changes to the syllabus during class. Accommodations that provide for them to be given written instructions will eliminate the potentially disastrous problems that could otherwise result from this processing issue. Students who struggle with oral presentations can ask for an accommodation that allows them either to make a written presentation, or to do an oral presentation privately with the professor. Clearly, the more familiar students become with their particular challenges, the more control they will have over their success.

All post-secondary education (PSE) institutions require some type of documentation to support the student's need for accommodations and to confirm the nature of the student's disability. As discussed, it's a good idea to communicate with the Disabilities Services Office (DSO) ahead of time to determine what type of testing might be required— usually a recent, complete psychological or neuropsychological evaluation and report by a licensed psychologist. The report should contain a description of the student's disability, learning style, strengths and weaknesses, and recommended accommodations. It's important to refer the family to a psychologist who is familiar with this type of evaluation (and with ASD), and who can write a report that will not only secure the appropriate accommodations, but also provide a strong overview of the student's needs. The cost of this evaluation is borne by the family. However, it is a valuable endeavor for many reasons apart from obtaining accommodations. The psychologist who conducts the evaluation can review the findings with the student. In terms of self-awareness and self-advocacy, this process helps students understand the types of accommodations that will be helpful, and why, based on their performance and the professional's observations. This knowledge places students in a better position to advocate for their needs in the college setting.

A neuropsychological battery of tests can consist of a number of different instruments designed to assess how an individual's brain functions. Tests are selected based on why the individual is being referred for testing. In this case, the purpose of an evaluation is to identify the kinds of accommodations the student will need in college. Therefore, test selection should focus on the following: overall cognitive and academic abilities; learning style; all aspects of memory (short- and long-term, working memory, visual/auditory memory, etc.); problem-solving; mood, anxiety, and other emotional issues; attention and focus; visual-motor functioning; motor speed; spatial reasoning; receptive and expressive language concerns; verbal and nonverbal fluency; verbal/auditory learning; reasoning; judgment; executive functions; organization; flexibility of thinking; and abstract thinking. Additional areas that would be important to evaluate include: adaptive functioning; independence; sensory challenges; social skills; Theory of Mind skills; and coping skills.

Below are two lists of accommodations. The first is a list of standard accommodations typically available at most colleges to students with learning disabilities. The second is a list of additional accommodations that benefit students with ASD in particular.

Standard accommodations (most students with learning disabilities)

- note taker
- extra time for tests
- tests in quiet location

- modified assignments (but cannot compromise academic requirements)
- tutoring: peer, staff, and/or cost-based
- study skills
- academic mentoring
- assistive technology
- computer lab
- help with course selection
- advance registration
- pass/fail or credit/no credit courses.

Specific accommodations for students with ASD

- assistance with time management, including prioritizing, and dealing with procrastination
- learning self-limiting skills for dealing with specific interests in computer, video games, or internet
- breaking course loads down into smaller, more manageable chunks
- using visual schedules and sequences for chunking, especially with long-term assignments
- voice recognition software for dictation of papers
- help with organizing class materials
- using visual and concrete supports for understanding instructions
- checking for understanding of instructions, and/or clarification of material, on a regular basis until it is clear that understanding is adequate
- use of "priming" to prepare for next class/lecture (e.g. providing student with advance notice of what will be covered next; giving student notes for the current or next class)
- study skills training
- specific guidance for working in groups
- intervening as needed to develop appropriate classroom behavior and reduce inappropriate behavior (correcting professor, asking too many questions, thought broadcasting)

- allowing sensory breaks where student leaves the classroom for short periods of time, as needed, to deal with sensory issues
- mitigating the distraction caused by fluorescent lights and noisy corridors (e.g. wear sunglasses/tinted glasses; headphones for sound dampening, so long as student is still able to hear the lecture)
- single dorm room
- removal of fluorescent lighting in dorm room
- social mentoring to help deal with bullying, social manipulation, dating issues, personal space, eye contact
- guidance in managing roommate issues: neatness, overnight dates, drugs/alcohol, sharing responsibilities in the room
- advocacy training: communicate needs to professors; disclose disability to other students; dealing with public safety
- assistance finding appropriate activities/clubs, support groups, or student organizations for students with disabilities
- managing independent living skills (e.g. money management, hygiene, health and fitness)
- referrals available for professional "coaches"
- on-campus counseling, free or cost-based.

ADDITIONAL SUPPORTS AND TEACHING STRATEGIES

Familiarity is what helps students with ASD feel comfortable. The more familiar they can be with their environment, their professors, the expectations of others around them, etc., the less stress they will experience. A few things students can do to develop familiarity are:

- visit and become familiar with the campus prior to starting school
- visit all assigned classrooms before classes start
- arrive to class early on the first day of class to meet the professor and possibly discuss disability needs
- make contact with and, if possible, arrange to meet with roommate prior to moving in
- meet and talk with disabilities advisor prior to classes beginning
- ask for a written version of the unwritten rules of the classroom, dorm, and campus environments.

In terms of teaching strategies, it is important for professors to remember the following:

- Use fewer words when explaining assignments. Some students may be highly verbal, but that doesn't mean their receptive language skills match.

- Sarcasm, innuendos and/or double meanings in lectures and literature may confuse the student. Be sure to check for understanding, and if necessary provide clarification.

- Provide a clear syllabus of course assignments, when tests will be given, and the nature of each lecture.

- When changes to the syllabus happen, alert the student ahead of time, individually, and in writing.

- Make time to meet with the student on a weekly basis. These meetings will go a long way towards helping the student feel comfortable with each professor, which will, in turn, help the student feel more comfortable on campus.

Chapter 11

ARE WE READY?

For the most part, the current generation of students with ASD has benefited from various levels of intensive early intervention, ongoing remediation, and support services throughout their primary and secondary educations. It is they who will teach us how to improve early intervention and determine what other strategies are needed over their course of development to ensure a successful outcome. We don't know yet what the benefits of intervention are to the older student and adult, and this is a ripe area for research.

What we do know at this point is that many adults with ASD struggle to live independently and to find satisfactory employment. They also continue to struggle interpersonally. While we are preparing students for success in primary, elementary, and secondary school, there is a significant gap in the various service delivery systems available to further an individual's progress once he or she gets out of high school. Other types of interventions, as well as modifications to current interventions, are needed to help students develop skills that will ultimately mean less hands-on supervision in college and in the workplace.

One of the most challenging aspects of post-secondary education (PSE), which has been observed for students with ASD who have attempted college so far, lies in the area of independent living skills (ILS) and self-management. In California, the Department of Disabilities and state Regional Centers for Individuals with Disabilities do not begin ILS instruction until the "consumer" (the term used for individuals who qualify for their services) reaches the age of 18. Some Regional Centers will not authorize these services until six months before the "consumer" is planning to move out of their parents' home. If students with ASD are going to attend college upon graduation from high school, it is necessary for school districts and other state and federal agencies to work towards helping *younger* students develop these very important and necessary skills *before* they graduate from high school.

Currently, high schools approach preparing students with disabilities for their future plans, including PSE, via the student's Transition Plan. The United States Department of Education's Institute of Education Services (IES) (2009) recently made five recommendations for how high schools can help students find their way to college. They suggest that high schools "offer courses and curricula that prepare students for college-level work, and ensure that students understand what constitutes a college-ready curriculum by ninth grade" (p.iii). According to the Individuals with Disabilities Education Act (IDEA) 2004, a formal Transition Plan is to be written no later than the student's sixteenth birthday, but can also begin prior to this time. Beginning the process in ninth grade will be of enormous benefit to students with ASD. As well as making students aware of what college-level work looks like, the IES also recommends that high schools assess students' readiness throughout high school "so that students are aware of how prepared they are for college, and assist them in overcoming deficiencies as they are identified" (p.iii). This kind of assessment will be crucial for students with ASD, who may have minimal awareness of what is required in the college setting, and of their own particular areas of strength and weakness. Students also need a support network of "adults and peers who can support their college-going aspirations" (p.iii)—again, a very important element for students with ASD. If implemented correctly, this model can also serve to prepare students for interacting with peer and adult mentors in college. In conjunction with high-school staff, this support network also serves the purpose of helping students participate in "completing critical steps for college entry" (p.iii). Finally, the IES report recommends that high schools "increase families' financial awareness, and help students apply for financial aid" (p.iii). More detailed and supporting data are offered in the body of this extensive report. There are many current programs offering scholarships for individuals with disabilities, and it is likely that others will be created in the future. High schools can also offer students with disabilities a number of online resources for them to learn more about the college experience (see Appendix B).

Similarly, PSE institutions face their own challenges. According to a recent report by the United States Government Accountability Office (2009), "schools face challenges in supporting students who are unaware of their rights and responsibilities regarding accommodations and in providing services that involve specialized knowledge" (p.1). Faculty members also need to be educated about their legal responsibilities in working with students with disabilities. At the governmental level the report "recommends that the Secretary of Education develop and implement a coordinated approach to optimize agency resources and knowledge in providing technical assistance to postsecondary schools in supporting students with disabilities" (p.1). While it may take some time for all agencies and institutions to update and modify their approaches, their efforts will enable more students with disabilities to maximize their potential.

CURRENT STATE OF AFFAIRS

The most recent study (Kogan *et al.* 2009) aimed at determining current prevalence rates of ASD in the United States was published by *Pediatrics*, the official journal of the American Academy of Pediatrics. The authors re-examined the findings of the "2007 National Survey of Children's Health (sample size: 78,037)" and found that the incidence of ASD in children between three and seventeen years of age "is higher than previous US estimates" (p.1). Based on their findings, prevalence rates of ASD in 2009 are one in 91, compared to the prevalence rates of one in 150 previously reported by the Centers for Disease Control and Prevention (CDC) in 2007. What this means is that approximately 1 percent of children are being diagnosed with ASD. On 5 October 2009 (the day the study in *Pediatrics* was published and posted on the internet), the CDC published a statement confirming that their findings were consistent with those of Kogan *et al.* An updated prevalence report from the CDC is expected to be published before the end of 2009.

According to Gerhardt (2009b), ASD is "more common than pediatric cancer, diabetes, and AIDS combined" (p.2).

In 2006 a survey of families of adults with ASD who were no longer in the school system by the Indiana Resource Center for Autism (IRCA) "showed that 65% of people over age 18 represented in the survey were unemployed, 14% worked in sheltered workshops and 25% worked in community jobs" (Pratt 2007). Of those who were employed, their median annual income was approximately $6,500. Findings from other studies are similar. Contrast these findings with reports from the US Department of Labor noting that "89% of [neurotypical] college graduates ages 25–34 are a part of the civilian labor force" and "the remaining 11% enter graduate school, stay home to raise a family or enter the military" (VanBergeijk *et al.* 2008).

The California State Department of Developmental Disabilities recently reported that by the end of 2009 their Regional Centers anticipate providing services to more than 50,000 individuals with autism (Hubert 2009). Hubert further states, "If the trend continues, that number will grow to 70,000 by June 2012… Nationally, the number of autistic children expected to need extensive adult services by 2023 is about 380,000 people, and the bill for caring for them will be in the billions of dollars" (p.1).

These statistics are alarming. As a society we *must* find a way to address these issues, and we are running out of time. There is already ample anecdotal and statistical support for the fact that countless numbers of individuals—at all levels of functioning—have not received services and supports that would enable them to be productive members of society. According to Holmes (2007), "The problem lies in two areas: the lack of proper preparation for work *during the education years* and the lack of laws and funding to entitle adults with disabilities to the same rights established for children under IDEA (Individuals with Disabilities Education Improvement Act of 2004). Both areas must be addressed immediately, if America is to stem the tide of unemployment among its citizens with disabilities" (p.17; emphasis added).

In response to these important concerns, the organization Advancing Futures for Adults with Autism (AFAA) was formed. A think tank session was convened in January 2009 to address the paucity of services for adults with ASD and determine the types of modifications and interventions that are needed for adults with ASD to become "engaged active citizens and lead lives of competence, quality and dignity." In advance of this important meeting, Gerhardt (2009a) prepared and presented an extensive report, *The Current State of Services for Adults with Autism*, in which gaps in the provision and availability of services geared towards "housing, employment and community integration" were identified. Gerhardt notes that:

> The group of people with autism spectrum disorder (ASD) diagnosed as part of the first wave of what is typically referred to as the autism epidemic is rapidly approaching adulthood. This group represents only the proverbial tip of the iceberg. Some reports noting that 70% of the identified individuals with ASD are less than 14 years old. This is a looming crisis of unprecedented magnitude for adults with ASD, their families, and the ill-prepared and under-funded adult service system charged with meeting their needs. (p.3)

Below is an overview of the results, as stated at the beginning of this important document.

- Outcome studies of adults with ASD document that, independent of current ability levels, the vast majority of adults with ASD are either unemployed or underemployed.

- The majority of adults with autism continue to live with parents, siblings or older relatives.

- The current economic slowdown can be expected to have a direct, and negative, impact on the availability of adult services.

- For many individuals with ASD, the transition requirements of IDEA are poorly implemented with little attention to service coordination or direct family involvement.

- The Federal Department of Health and Human Services indicates that combined, annual average staff turnover rate for programs serving adults with developmental disabilities is 50% coupled with a staff vacancy rate of 10–12%.

- While appropriate and effective residential and employment models exist, access to these models is greatly restricted, due primarily to a lack of adequate funding.

- The smaller the unit of service (e.g., individual supervised living or customized employment) the greater the likelihood for community integration.

- There is a great need for programs, services, and naturally occurring supports for such critical aspects of adult life as personal safety, transportation, leisure, health/wellness, and sexuality.

- The greatest impediments to development of integrated lives of quality and dignity for adults with autism are system inadequacies coupled with a public perception of adults on the spectrum being unemployable.

(Gerhardt 2009, p.3)

The question posed in the title of this chapter, "Are we ready?," is critical. We *must* find a way to address systemic failures and inadequacies if we are to keep the rising costs of care for individuals with ASD manageable. Current cost estimates suggest that the direct and indirect cost of medical and non-medical services combined is somewhere upwards of $35 billion (Gaus 2007, reported in Gerhardt 2009a). These costs will only increase with the ever increasing numbers of individuals being diagnosed with ASD.

There is a consensus among professionals, service providers, and educators that significant systemic and practical changes need to happen at both the secondary and post-secondary level so that students with ASD can be successful in college and later in life. However, I believe that with more careful consideration the provision of services at even younger ages will go a long way towards lessening the burden and intensity of services needed at the secondary level, and will be more effective in developing personal independence and life fulfillment in individuals with ASD. However, the process of implementing change is encumbered by funding shortages and the more sophisticated levels of training needed to make effective instructional and environmental shifts so that the complex information-processing and social challenges of students with ASD can be met.

While many students with ASD have been and will continue to be successful in a traditional PSE setting with appropriate supports, there are a significant number of students who, while able to handle the academic aspects of a PSE experience, will struggle or be unable to keep up in most other ways. With the latter in mind, intervention teams at the secondary level can implement a number of strategies in school, home, and community settings (as discussed in this book) in an effort to initiate the preparation process *prior* to the student's graduation from high school.

Post-secondary transition programs are also needed to meet the needs of some of these students. There are already a handful of excellent transition programs available, but many of them can be quite costly for most families, and the ones that are not have waiting lists of more than three years. Finding a way to fund these programs so that more students can have access to them is a challenge that can be taken on immediately. What ultimately needs to happen is a combination of state, insurance, and personal financial support for various segments of the transitional program. A three-part funding concept is offered below.

- State disability agencies can contribute to funding the independent living components of the program.

- Personal insurance and/or state-funded insurance programs can contribute to the costs for the social/emotional components of the program.

- Parents can consider funding the educational/remediation components by means of out-of-pocket funds, college savings, grants, or loans.

The cost to parents and families is great, and perhaps over time more grant programs and scholarships will evolve. However, the cost to society of not finding a way to ensure that students with ASD can attend college and be successful will be enormous and potentially devastating.

Most good post-secondary transition programs offer the following components. Please refer to Part II for specific skills in each area.

Residential/independent living skills component

- residential capability where students live either in apartments with a roommate, or in a dorm-like setting

- daily instruction in and supervision of independent living skills, including environmental and personal hygiene; strategies for managing personal sensory challenges; self-care; and dealing with unexpected problem situations in the home or community.

Social/emotional component

- social engagement facilitation in a group setting
- ongoing development of more sophisticated Theory of Mind skills
- personal problem-solving strategies with roommates and classmates
- psychotherapy to address self-awareness, self-advocacy, asking for help, and dating/relationship issues.

Educational/remediation component

- developing and maintaining routines
- flexibility in thinking and planning
- executive functioning skills as they affect life and academics.

While it may be difficult for transition programs to offer individualized programming based on student need, they should make it available to the best of their ability, bearing in mind that not all students will require intervention in all of the above-mentioned areas. Allocating only those services needed by a particular student may also help to minimize costs.

Most existing transition programs have begun to offer summer camps for high-school juniors and seniors, and I strongly encourage parents to enroll their students in these programs, for a number of reasons. It may, in fact, be the first time the student has been away from his parents for any extended period of time, and the experience of doing so and succeeding can bolster his sense of independence and self-confidence. This experience can also serve as a wake-up call and model for students who may not yet have a realistic handle on their strengths and weaknesses. Being away from home and accountable to adults other than one's parents can be a great learning experience for students with ASD. Parents tend to be more lenient and accommodating to their children than other adults ever will be, and the level of accountability and responsibility that is expected of students when they go away to any camp (or college) is often alien to them. While this experience can be quite shocking, it is also extremely valuable.

ROADBLOCKS

In addition to the funding and practical issues outlined above, there is another significant roadblock to accessing appropriate levels of services for high functioning individuals with ASD. Many service delivery systems in the US (e.g. Department of Disabilities, public education, Vocational Rehabilitation) currently operate on a philosophical and practical model that focuses on meeting the needs of lower functioning individuals. The Developmental Disabilities Act was created in 1970, and autism was not included in it until 1975 (Sullivan 1979). Holmes (2007) notes that while autism was included under the Developmental Disabilities Act more than 20 years ago, most people with autism with an IQ of less than 70 continue to be serviced under departments overseeing individuals with mental retardation. However, individuals with ASD at all functioning levels present with different kinds of challenges. Service coordinators who authorize services, and the vendors who provide the services, need ongoing, updated and specific training in ASD, particularly at the higher functioning (HF) range. This kind of training has already begun at some levels. However, the institution of contemporary and appropriate services can be mired in programmatic and budgetary restrictions. As a result, these services are not always available to the individuals who need them.

Not only do these issues affect public schools and state developmental disabilities agencies, they also permeate into departments of vocational rehabilitation. Vocational rehabilitation (VR) services in the US are governed and funded by Title I of the Rehabilitation Act of 1973. VR services are "designed to enable participants to attain skills, resources, attitudes, and expectations needed to find and keep employment... help someone retrain for employment after injury or mental disorder has disrupted previous employment..." (Johnson 2007, p.10). The ultimate goal of VR services is to enable individuals with disabilities to "obtain gainful employment in integrated settings" (p.11). However, there are countless incidents of individuals being offered positions that are significantly below their functioning capabilities (e.g. working in a factory sorting objects, food service preparation, janitorial work, dishwashing). While jobs for higher functioning individuals may not be plentiful, it is also likely that lack of training and experience in working with HF individuals limits the VR counselor's ability to identify appropriate employment. The impact of these experiences on individuals with ASD is great. The person may be hurt or insulted beyond repair, and almost always begins to question his functioning level, which can destroy an already fragile sense of self. Most important, however, is that the individual loses trust in the service delivery systems that are supposedly there to help, and is once again faced with a lack of appropriate services and supports.

According to Zimmerman (2008), "of the 36,952 people with autism [in the state of California] now receiving disability services from the state, 31,376—84 percent—are younger than age 21" (p.1). Children who received a diagnosis in the HF range in 1994 were somewhere between the ages of two and eight years, and sometimes older. Today, these individuals have either reached or are nearing college age. Investing in programs that help people with ASD lead independent lives and become taxpaying citizens "is a good value to the taxpayers who will see lower social welfare costs, additional taxpaying workers, and lower costs for other state services" (Duncan 2009). Indeed, the Transition to Independent Living (TIL) program at Taft College in California has proved that this can be accomplished and supports the efficacy and benefit of such an investment. Duncan (2009) notes that after a ten-year tracking of their graduates, "95% of TIL graduates live independently, 93% are competitively employed (the national average is 14%), 93% receive no financial assistance from other agencies or their families, 97% report that they are satisfied with their adult life, 30 hours of home assistance is provided on average each month (the state average is 88 hours per month)" (p.2).

CONCLUSION

Many individuals with ASD have already attempted study at higher education institutions—some successfully, while others are unable to complete their studies for various reasons. While most students have the grades to get accepted to four-year colleges or universities, getting accepted is only the first step. For students with ASD the college experience is more about how successfully they can fit in and function independently, rather than whether they have the cognitive skills to complete college coursework (Pantak 2007). Not only are the social expectations attached to being in a college environment complex, sophisticated, and demanding, the diversity of issues students with ASD bring to dorms, classrooms, and interpersonal relationships make the PSE experience daunting, at best. Students with ASD can succeed in post-high school vocational or educational endeavors when their unique challenges are addressed and supported. Employees with ASD are dependable, consistent, and highly focused on their work. The "social enterprise business model" (see Austin, Wareham and Busquets 2008; *Independent* 2005) is being used with increasing frequency by corporations small and large who are interested in promoting social responsibility and "person-centered activities" (*Independent* 2005) while simultaneously establishing and maintaining a solid and profitable company. Companies interested in hiring and training individuals with ASD value the precision, focus, and speed with which they perform tasks (Bennett 2009; *PR Web* 2009). Grandin (2004) notes that the charge of individuals with ASD is to "become so good at what we do that employers can't afford to let us go" (p.40). In fact, this is good advice for anyone in the workplace.

It is our responsibility as a society to make it possible for individuals with ASD to be all that they potentially can be, whether they go to college or otherwise. If we are unsuccessful, we will be doing them a great disservice, and we will also pay the price of supporting them throughout their lives. If we are successful, we will reap the benefits of their unique talents and distinctive qualities. The first generation of students entering college within the next five to seven years may struggle because we have only just begun to understand the prerequisite skills for future success. However, a joint effort between federal and state agencies and primary, secondary, and post-secondary schools to identify and make the necessary changes in service delivery and provision will make it easier for future generations of students with ASD to make their dreams come true.

REFERENCES

Adreon, D. and Durocher, J.S. (2007) "Evaluating the college transition needs of individuals with high-functioning autism spectrum disorders." Available at www.accessmylibrary.com/article-1G1-163197777/evaluating-college-transition-needs.html, accessed on 22 January 2010.

American Psychiatric Association (1994a) *Diagnostic and Statistical Manual of Mental Disorders, Fourth Edition* (DSM-IV). Washington, DC: APA.

American Psychiatric Association (1994b) *Quick Reference to the Diagnostic Criteria from DSM-IV*. Washington, DC: APA.

American Psychiatric Association (2000) *Diagnostic and Statistical Manual of Mental Disorders, Fourth Edition, Text Revision* (DSM-IV TR). Washington, DC: APA.

Attwood, S. (2008) *Making Sense of Sex: A Forthright Guide to Puberty, Sex and Relationships for People with Asperger's Syndrome*. London: Jessica Kingsley Publishers.

Attwood, T. (2007) *The Complete Guide to Asperger's Syndrome*. London: Jessica Kingsley Publishers.

Austin, R., Wareham, J. and Busquets, J. (2008) *Specialisterne: Sense and Details*. Harvard Business Publishing. Available at http://cb.hbsp.harvard.edu, accessed on 19 October 2009.

Barnard, L., Muldoon, K., Hasan, R., O'Brien, G. and Stewart, M. (2008) "Profiling executive dysfunction in adults with autism and comorbid learning disability." *Autism 12*, 2, 125–141.

Bennett, D. (2009) "Thorkil Sonne: Recruit autistics." *Wired Magazine*. Available at www.wired.com, accessed on 19 October 2009.

Bliss, V. and Edmonds, G. (2008) *A Self-Determined Future with Asperger Syndrome: Solution-Focused Approaches*. London: Jessica Kingsley Publishers.

Bodnar, J. (2005) *Raising Money Smart Kids: What They Need to Know About Money and How to Tell Them (Kiplinger's Personal Finance)*. Chicago, IL: Dearborn Trade Publishing.

Centers for Disease Control and Prevention (2007) Available at www.cdc.gov.mmwr/preview/mmwrhtml/ss5601a1.htm, accessed on 22 January 2010.

Chew, K. (2007) "Some thoughts on teaching college students on the spectrum." Available at www.blisstree.com/articles/some-thoughts-on-teaching-college-students-on-the-spectrum, accessed on 3 December 2009.

Chitale, R. (2008) "The dangers of autism—autism in America: a perilous diagnosis." *ABC News*. Available at http://abcnews.go.com, accessed on 8 November 2008.

Coulter, D. (2008) "Future prepping your child." Available at www.coultervideo.com, accessed on 3 November 2008.

Coulter, J. (2003) "First year of college: lessons learned." Available at www. pathfindersforautism.org/articleItem.aspx?id=20, accessed on 15 July 2006.

Crane, L. and Goddard, L. (2008) "Episodic and semantic autobiographical memory in adults with autism spectrum disorders." *Journal of Autism and Developmental Disorders 38,* 498–506.

Crane, L., Goddard, L. and Pring, L. (2009) "Sensory processiong in adults with autism spectrum disorders." *Autism 13,* 3, 215–228.

Dawson, P. and Guare, R. (2004) *Executive Skills in Children and Adolescents: A Practical Guide to Assessment and Intervention.* New York, NY: The Guilford Press.

Delis, D.C., Houston, W.S., Wetter, S., Han, S.D., Jacobson, M., Holdnack, J. and Kramer, J. (2007) "Creativity lost: The importance of testing higher-level executive functions in school-age children and adolescents." *Journal of Psychoeducational Assessment 25,* 1, 29–40.

Dubin, N. (2005) *Breaking Through Hidden Barriers.* Kentwood, MI: The Gray Center for Social Learning and Understanding.

Duncan, W. (2009) "Taft College Community College Consortium for autism and developmental disabilities: Helping autism students help themselves be part of the workforce." *The Taft Independent.* Available at www.taftindependent.com, accessed on 14 August 2009.

Dutton, M.K. (2008) "Autistic students get help navigating college life." *USA Today.* Available at www.usatoday.com, accessed on 8 July 2008.

Dziobek, I., Rogers, K., Fleck, S., Bahnemann, M., Heekeren, H.R., Wolf, O.T. and Convit, A. (2008) "Dissociation of cognitive and emotional empathy in adults with Asperger's syndrome using the Multifaceted Empathy Test (MET)." *Journal of Autism and Developmental Disorders 38,* 464–473.

Egan, M. (2005) "Students with Asperger's syndrome in the CS classroom." Available at http://portal.acm.org, accessed on 30 September 2008.

Evans, B. (2008) "Marshall program teaches independent living skills." *The Parthenon.* Available at www.marshallparthenon.com, accessed on 27 January 2010.

Faherty, C. (2002) "Asperger's syndrome in women: a different set of challenges?"Available at www.udel.edu, accessed on 1 October 2009.

Freedman, S. (2001) "High functioning autism/Asperger's syndrome: diagnostic dilemmas and impact on the family." *Autism Asperger's Digest,* November/December, 28–31.

Freedman, S. (2007) "Adults on the spectrum: college and beyond." *Los Angeles County Psychologist,* November/December, 13–14.

Frith, U. (1989) *Autism. Explaining the Enigma.* Oxford: Blackwell.

Frith, U. and Happe, F. (1994) "Autism: beyond 'Theory of Mind.'" *Cognition 50,* 115–132.

Gaus, V.L. (2007) *Cognitive Behavioral Therapy for Adult Asperger Syndrome.* New York, NY: The Guilford Press.

Gerhardt, P. (2009a) "The current state of services for adults with autism." Organization for Autism Research. Available at http://nyc4a.org, accessed on 1 October 2009.

Gerhardt, P. (2009b) "Advancing futures for adults with autism 2009 think tank." Organization for Autism Research. Available at www.afaa-us.org, accessed on 1 October 2009.

Gilotty, L., Kenworthy, L., Sirian, L., Black, D. and Wagner, A. (2002) "Adaptive skills and executive function in autism spectrum disorders." *Child Neuropsychology 8*, 4, 241–248.

Gioia, G., Isquith, P., Guy, S. and Kenworthy, L. (2000) *Behavior Rating Inventory of Executive Function, Professional Manual.* Florida, CA: Psychological Assessment Resources, Inc.

Godfrey, N., Edwards, C. and Richards, T. (2006) *Money Doesn't Grow on Trees: A Parent's Guide to Raising Financially Responsible Children.* New York, NY: Fireside.

Graetz, J. and Spampinato, K. (2008) "Asperger's syndrome and the voyage through high school: Not the final frontier." *Journal of College Admission* (Winter), 198. Available at http://findarticles.com/p/articles/mi_qa3955/is_200801/ai_n24394187/?tag=content;col1, accessed on 28 February 2010.

Grandin, T. (2004) *Developing Talents: Careers for Individuals with Asperger Syndrome and High-Functioning Autism.* Shawnee Mission, KS: Autism Asperger Publishing Company.

Grandin, T. and Barron, S. (2005) *Unwritten Rules of Social Relationships: Decoding Social Mysteries Through the Unique Perspectives of Autism.* Arlington, TX: Future Horizons.

Gray, C. (1998) "Social stories and comic strip conversations with students with Asperger Syndrome and high functioning autism." In E. Schopler, G.B. Mesibov and L. Kunce (eds) *Asperger Syndrome and High Functioning Autism.* New York, NY: Plenum Press.

Guerrero, L.K., Anderson, P.A. and Afifi, W.A. (2007) *Close Encounters: Communication in Relationships.* (Second edition.) London: Sage Publications, Inc.

Hand, R. and Paradiz, V. (2009) "The culture of autism." *Autism Advocate*, first edition, April 2009.

Harpur, J., Lawlor, M. and Fitzgerald, M. (2004) *Succeeding in College with Asperger Syndrome: A Student Guide.* London: Jessica Kingsley Publishers.

Hoekman, L. (2008) "Independent living." *Gray Center SUN News.* Available at http://graycenter.wordpress.com, accessed on 7 July 2008.

Holmes, D. (2007) "When the school bus stops coming: the employment dilemma for adults with autism." *Autism Advocate 46*, first edition, 16–20.

Howlin, P., Baron-Cohen, S. and Hadwin, J. (1999) *Teaching Children with Autism to Mind-read: A Practical Guide.* Chichester: John Wiley and Sons.

Hubert, C. (2009) "Rise in autistic adults worries caregivers." *The Sacramento Bee.* Available at www.sacbee.com.

Hume, K., Loftin, R. and Lantz, J. (2009) "Increasing independence in autism spectrum disorders: A review of three focused interventions." *Journal of Autism & Developmental Disorders 39*, 2, 1329–1338.

Independent, The (2005) "The social enterprise business model is a proven means of developing people-centered activities." Available at www.nextbillion.net, accessed on 3 November 2009.

Individuals with Disabilities Education Improvement Act of 2004, 20 U.S.C. [section] 1400 *et seq.* (2004) (Reauthorization of the Individuals with Disabilities Education Act of 1990.) Available at http://idea.ed.gov, accessed on 1 October 2009.

Iland, E.D. (2008) "What is reading?" *Café Autism.* Available at www.cafeautism.com, accessed on 15 July 2008.

Interlandi, J. (2008) "More than just quirky." *Newsweek Web Exclusive.* Available at www. newsweek.com, accessed on 13 November 2008.

Irlen, H. (1998) *The Irlen Method—Helping Children and Adults with Processing Problems for over 25 years.* Available at http://irlen.com/index.php, accessed on 17 December 2009.

Jobe, L.E. and White, S.W. (2007) "Loneliness, social relationships, and a broader autism phenotype in college students." *Personality and Individual Differences 42,* 8, 1479–1489.

Johnson, C. (2007) "Getting to Work: The Rehabilitation Act and the vocational rehabilitation system." *Autism Advocate 46,* first edition, 54–57.

Johnson, K. and Hines, T. (2005) *100 Things Every College Student with a Disability Ought to Know.* Williamsville, NY: The Cambridge Stratford Study Skills Institute.

Klin, A., Volkmar, F.R. and Sparrow, S.S. (eds.) (2000) *Asperger Syndrome.* New York: Guilford Press.

Knapp, M.L. (1978) *Social Intercourse: From Greeting to Goodbye.* Boston. MA: Allyn and Bacon.

Knapp, M.L. and Vangelisti, A.L. (2005) *Interpersonal Communication and Human Relationships.* (Fifth edition.) Boston, MA: Allyn and Bacon.

Kogan, M.D., Blumberg, S.J., Schieve, L.A., Boyle, C.A., Perrin, J.M., Ghandour, R.M., Singh, G.K., Strickland, B.B., Trevathan, E. and vanDyck, P.C. (2009) "Prevalence of parent-reported diagnosis of autism spectrum disorder among children in the US, 2007." *Pediatrics* DOI: 10.1542/peds.2009–1522. Published online on 5 October 2009, available at http://pediatrics.aappublications.org, accessed on 5 October 2009.

Korpi, M. (2008) *Guiding Your Teenager with Special Needs Through the Transition from School to Adult Life: Tools for Parents.* London: Jessica Kingsley Publishers.

McCurrach, D. (2003) *Allowance Magic: Turn Your Kids Into Money Wizards.* Franklin, TN: Kid's Money Press.

Mayer, J.D., Salovey, P. and Caruso, D.R. (2008) "Emotional intelligence." *American Psychologist 63,* 6, 503–517.

Mitchell, P. and O'Keefe, K. (2008) "Brief report: Do individuals with autism spectrum disorder think they know their own minds?" *Journal of Autism and Developmental Disorders 38,* 1591–1597.

Moore, A.S. (2006) "A dream not denied: students on the spectrum." *New York Times.* Available at www.nytimes.com, accessed on 28 September 2008.

Newmarker, C. (2008) "The world is their classroom: Princeton encourages student travel." *The Kansas City Star.* Available at www.kansascity.com, accessed on 31 March 2008.

Page, T. (2007) "Parallel play." *The New Yorker,* 20 August 2007, 36–41.

Palmer, A. (2006) *Realizing the College Dream with Asperger Syndrome: A Parent's Guide to Student Success.* London: Jessica Kingsley Publishers.

Pantak, M. (2007) "On the cover: alone with autism." *State Press Magazine.* Available at www.cal-dsa.org, accessed on 31 October 2007.

Perner, L. (2007) "Preparing to be nerdy where nerdy can be cool: college planning for the high functioning student with autism." *USC Marshall.* Available at www. professorsadvice.com.

Perry, N. (2009) *Adults on the Autism Spectrum Leave the Nest.* London: Jessica Kingsley Publishers.

Pratt, C. (2007) "Moving into the World of Employment." *Autism Advocate 46,* first edition, 36–41.

Prince-Hughes, D. (2002) *Aquamarine Blue.* Athens, OH: Shallow Press/Ohio University Press.

PR Web (2009) "Gary Rosenthal combines business, art, and social responsibility in new 'woven collection' with the help of special needs employees." Available at www.prweb. com, accessed on 3 November 2009.

Richard, G.J. and Fahy, J.K. (2005) *The Source for Development of Executive Functions.* Illinois, IL: LinguiSystems.

Safos, B. (2008) "Almost 50 years old and diagnosed with autism." Available at www.wkyc. com, accessed on 1 October 2009.

Shore, S.M. and Rastelli, L.G. (2006) *Understanding Autism for Dummies.* Hoboken, NJ: Wiley Publishing, Inc.

Sicile-Kira, C. (2008) "Autism life skills." Available at www.awares.org, accessed on 30 November 2009.

SmartStart: "Decisions about graduation." Available at www.special-ed-law.com /Brief%20 Bank5g7jr/Graduation.pdf, accessed on 5 October 2009.

Solove, D. (2006) "A guide to grading exams." Available at www.concurringopinions.com, accessed on 14 July 2008.

Sperry, L.A. and Mesibov, G.B. (2005) "Perceptions of social challenges of adults with autism spectrum disorder." *Autism 9,* 4, 362–376.

Sterling, L., Dawson, G., Estes, A. and Greenson, J. (2008) "Characteristics associated with the presence of depressive symptoms in adults with autism spectrum disorder." *Journal of Autism and Developmental Disorders 38,* 1011–1018.

Sullivan, R.C. (1979) "The politics of definitions: How autism got included in the Developmental Disabilities Act." *Journal of Autism and Developmental Disorders 9,* 2, June.

Trudeau, M. (2008) "An autistic student's journey to college." Available at www.npr.org, accessed on 24 September 2008.

Tse, J., Strulovitch, J., Tagalakis, V., Meng, L. and Fombonne, E. (2007) "Social skills training for adolescents with Asperger syndrome and high-functioning autism." *Journal of Autism and Developmental Disorders 37,* 1960–1968.

United States Department of Education, Institute of Education Sciences (2009) "Helping students navigate the path to college: what high schools can do." Available at http:// ies.ed.gov, accessed on 2 November 2009.

United States Government Accountability Office (2009) "Higher education and disability: education needs a coordinated approach to improve its assistance to schools in supporting students." Available at www.gao.gov, accessed on 2 November 2009.

VanBergeijk, E., Klin, A. and Volkmar, F. (2008) "Supporting more able students on the autism spectrum: college and beyond." *Journal of Autism and Developmental Disorders 38,* 1359–1370.

Willey, L. (1999) *Pretending to be Normal.* London: Jessica Kingsley Publishers.

Williams, D. (2008) "Autistic attachment: can those with autism experience love, loss and trauma?" Available at www.awares.org.

Wolf, L.E., Thierfeld Brown, J. and Kukiela Bork, R. (2009) *Students with Asperger's Syndrome: A Guide for College Personnel.* Shawnee Mission, KS: Autism Asperger Publishing Company.

Zimmerman, J. (2008) "As autistic children age, society faces challenges." *The Press Enterprise.* Available at www.pe.com, accessed on 22 March 2008.

Appendix A

OVERVIEW OF SKILL SETS

	Personal	Daily living	Academic issues	Executive functions
Environmental	• Sensory issues: noise, perfume, light, etc. in all campus environments • Creating sameness of setting day-to-day. • Creating study vs. leisure routines.	• Environmental hygiene. • Controlling mess. • Keeping clothes and personal belongings organized. • Using the phone. • Using the internet.		• Create sameness and establish new routines (including flexibility).
Self-advocacy	• Knowing how and who to tell: advisors, professors, RA, roommate, other pertinent people. • Asking for a mentor, tutor, coach, therapist, etc. to help with personal issues. • Asking for help to tell (language issues).		• Understand your learning style and needs. • Maximize personal strengths. • Balance interests in course selection. • Ask for needed accommodations. • Develop motivation for non-preferred topics. • Behave appropriately in classroom. • Learn about grading system and keep track of grades.	• Develop techniques to grasp the big picture concepts. • Learn to work in a group.

Organizing information	• Medical information. • Insurance forms. • Important addresses and phone numbers. • Pre-printed address labels for family. • Bank records. • Birthday listings.	• Making appointments. • Recording appointments. • Keeping appointments. • Canceling appointments when unable to make it. • Responding to email. • Manage study and leisure time (i.e. video games).		• Learn and use task planner. • Chop course material into manageable chunks. • Learn to break down, organize and sequence homework assignments. • Learn the rules of multi-tasking. • Learn to plan for possible change. • Learn research strategies for library and online research. • Learn to organize research findings.
Asking for help	• Understanding the role of other important people in one's life. • Developing a sense of reciprocity. • Learning how to know if one needs help. • Knowing who to ask. • Developing familiarity with school's bullying and teasing rules. • Dealing with emergencies and emergency workers.	• Identifying appropriate person to ask for help. • Befriending professors—meeting regularly with them. • Attending daily meetings with mentor, fading as appropriate.	• Identify individual professors' preference for asking questions. • Keep a record of each professor's office hours. • Communicate with professors by email when appropriate.	

Self-care	• Medication management: taking regularly and ordering timely refills. • Finding and meeting new physicians. • Environmental hygiene. • Laundry. • Caring for basic physiological needs to stay healthy (exercise, eating/cooking). • Money management.	• Taking public transportation (schedules, stops, cost). • Maintaining personal vehicle. • Parking rules—street and structures. • Accessing roadside assistance.		• Time management.
Self-awareness	• Self-acceptance. • Emotion and physical state recognition. • Linking and retrieving personal and emotional events. • Recognizing symptoms of depression and/or anxiety. • Managing depression. • Learning and practicing stress management techniques. • Knowing importance of getting psychological support. • Knowing where to get support on campus. • Knowing when/who to call for psychological support.	• Dealing with frustration with professors and peers. • Monitor sense of wasting time in college. • Learn to deal with different personalities—teachers and peers.		

Social	

Social	• Knowing how to protect yourself from exploitation. • Learning how to know when you're being taken advantage of. • Reading body language and other nonverbal cues and mental states. • Perspective-taking skills. • Showing empathy. • Dating issues. • Sex education and birth control	• Learn expectations about dating. • Learn expectations about marriage. • Learn difference between small talk and when someone is romantically interested. • Learn about dating and getting consent at every level of romantic advancement. • Learn to stop before being too pushy. • Learn how to encourage wanted and discourage unwanted advances.	• Classroom etiquette. • Manage emotional reactions to professors, peers, and college as whole. • Monitor sense of knowing more than others.	

Appendix B

RESOURCES

GENERAL AUTISM

Asperger Foundation International
www.aspfi.org

Asperger Syndrome and High Functioning Autism Association
www.ahany.org

Aspiefriends Listserve
http://groups.yahoo.com/group/Aspiefriends

ASPIRES
www.aspires-relationships.com
Online resources for spouses and family members of adults with ASD.

Auties.org
www.auties.org
Website for adults with Asperger's syndrome.

Autism Fitness
www.autismfitness.com

Autism Network International
www.autreat.com

Autism Risk and Safety Management
www.autismriskmanagement.com

Autistic Self-Advocacy Network (ASAN)
www.autisticadvocacy.org

Autism Society of America
www.autism-society.org

Autism Speaks
www.autismspeaks.org

Childnett.tv
www.childnett.tv
Autism TV on the internet.

Coping: a survival guide for people with Asperger Syndrome
www-users.cs.york.ac.uk/~alistair/survival
Article by Marc Segar, available on the University of York (UK) website.

The Daniel J. Fiddle Foundation
www.djfiddlefoundation.org
The Daniel Jordan Fiddle Foundation was established to develop, advocate for and support programs through grant awards that enrich the lives of adolescents and adults with autism spectrum disorders (ASD).

Families of Adults Affected by Asperger's Syndrome (FAAAS)
www.faaas.org

Family Travel and Autism
http://autismtravel.org

Global and Regional Asperger Syndrome
Partnership (GRASP)
www.grasp.org
Support group and information services for
adults with ASD.

National Autistic Society (UK)
www.autism.org.uk

National Dissemination Center for
Children with Disabilities (NICHCY)
www.nichcy.org
US national information center that provides
information on disabilities and disability
related issues, focusing on children and
youth.

National Institute of Mental Health
www.nimh.nih.gov

National Institute of Neurological
Disorders and Stroke (NINDS)
www.ninds.nih.gov

Online Asperger Syndrome Information
and Support Center (OASIS MAAP)
www.aspergersyndrome.org
Online Asperger's syndrome information
and support.

Treatment and Education of Autistic and
Communication Handicapped Children
(TEACCH)
www.teacch.com

Wrong Planet
www.wrongplanet.net
Online community and resource for those
with Asperger's syndrome.

US FEDERAL AND STATE ASSISTANCE AND GUIDELINES FOR COPING WITH ASD

The Americans with Disabilities Act
www.ada.gov

Federal Educational Rights and Privacy
Act (FERPA)
www.ferpa.gov

Section 504 of the Rehabilitation Act of
1973
www.ada.gov/cguide.htm#anchor65610

Social Security Administration
www.ssa.gov

US Department of Education, Office for
Civil Rights
www2.ed.gov/about/offices/list/ocr/
index.html

EDUCATIONAL INFORMATION AND ADVICE
General
Achieving in Higher Education with
Autism/Developmental Disabilities
(AHEADD)
www.aheadd.org
Cost-based consulting.

Asperger Syndrome Education Network
(ASPEN)
www.aspennj.org

Association on Higher Education and
Disability
www.ahead.org

Johnson O'Connor Research Foundation.
www.jocrf.org
Aptitude testing for career and educational
guidance. Offices in various cities in the US.

Organization for Autism Research (OAR)
www.researchautism.org

University Students with Autism and
Asperger's Syndrome
www.users.dircon.co.uk/~cns/index.html

US Department of Education, Office for
Civil Rights
www2.ed.gov/about/offices/list/ocr/
index.html

Preparing to go to college
Going to College
www.going-to-college.org
A resource for teens with disabilities.

Lars Perner
www.larsperner.com
General information about PSE and ASD.

TEACCH
www.teacch.com/college
Tips for students with HFA/ASD.

Think College
www.thinkcollege.net
Helps youth with intellectual disabilities
find out more about post-secondary
possibilities.

University of Washington
www.washington.edu/doit/Brochures/
Academics/cprep.html
"Preparing for college," an online tutorial;
internet resources for college-bound teens
with disabilities.

Self-assessment and study skills

Paragon Learning Style Inventory
www.oswego.edu/plsi

Vark
www.vark-learn.com
Tools for college students to recognize
learning style and acquire study skills.

Life skills

ADDitude Magazine
www.additudemag.com/adhd/article/1018
College survival tips for those with ADD/
ADHD.

Casey Life Skills
www.caseylifeskills.org
A free, online suite of easy-to-use tools
allows youth to assess their strengths in life
skills such as money management, work,
and study.

University of Melbourne
www.services.unimelb.edu/au/disability
See "Towards success in tertiary study with
Asperger's Syndrome and other Autistic
Spectrum Disorders," in particular. Available
at www.services.unimelb.edu.au/edp/
policy/success/aspergers.html#strategies.

Social skills

Coultervideo
www.coultervideo.com
Series of videotapes addressing various
social skills for high-school students with
ASD.

Gray Center
http://graycenter.wordpress.com
Resource for various articles, books, DVDs,
etc., including information on Social
Stories™ and Michelle Garcia Winner's
"Strategies for Organization" (DVD).

Social Thinking
www.socialthinking.com
Michelle Garcia Winner's website; good
resources for parents, clinicians, and
teachers.

TRANSITION PLANNING RESOURCES

Great Schools
www.greatschools.org/LD/school-
learning/transition-planning-for-students-
with-ieps.gs?content=873
Transition planning for students with
Individualized Education Plans (IEPs).

Jewish Childcare Association—Compass Project
www.jccany.org/site/DocServer/Compass_
brochure.pdf?docID=1101
High school to college transition.

National Secondary Transition Technical Assistance Center (NSTTAC)
www.nsttac.org
High school to college transition.

PACER Center
www.pacer.org/publications/index.asp
Handouts on transition, for parents.

The Youthhood
www.youthhood.org
Tool to help teens and adults plan for life
after high school.

Planning for transition to adulthood

My Future
www.myfuture.com
Assistance with career planning. Developed by the US Department of Defense, but has lots of great information not limited to a military career (as found in Korin 2007).

National Dissemination Center for Children with Disabilities (NICHCY)
www.nichcy.org/search/results.
aspx?k=transition%20to%20
adulthood&s=All%20OSEP%20
TA%26D%20Sites
Planning for transition to adulthood.

SCHOLARSHIPS FOR PEOPLE WITH DISABILITIES IN THE US

Autism and PDD Support Network
www.finaid.org/otheraid/disabled.phtml
Disability specific scholarships.

Autism Society of America
www.autism-society.org/site/
PageServer?pagename=asa_awards

The Collins Scholarship
Scholarship for people who want to study autism in their postdoctoral studies. Available through the Autism society of America (www.autism-society.org).

DisabilityScholarships.us
www.disabilityscholarships.us

Eden Services Charles H. Hoens Jr. Scholars Program
$1000 bursary for students with ASD who have been accepted to an accredited school. Can be used to pay for a degree or vocational program. Available through the Autism society of America (www.autism-society.org).

Doug Flutie Jr. Foundation for Autism
www.flutiefoundation.org
Offers scholarships for college-bound students with ASD.

Organization for Autism Research
www.sitelevel.com//query.go?crid=0c43e
8346ece6208&query=scholarships&x=0
&y=0
Research scholarship program.

BOOKS

Aresty, R. (2007) *How to Pay for College without Going Broke.* Available at http://ezinearticles.com/?How-To-Pay-For-College-Without-Going-Broke&id=523525, accessed on 3 March 2010.

Goldberg, D. and Zweibel, J. (2005) *The Organized Student: Teaching Children the Skills for Success in School and Beyond.* New York, NY: Fireside.

Gordon, M. and Keiser, S. (2000) (eds) *Accommodations in Higher Education Under the Americans with Disabilities Act.* New York, NY: GSI Publications.

Myles, B., Trautman, M. and Schelvan, R. (2004) *The Hidden Curriculum.* Shawnee Mission, KS: Autism Asperger Publishing Company.

Reiff, H.B. (2007) *Self-Advocacy Skills for Students with Learning Disabilities.* Port Chester, NY: Dude Publishing.

Robinson, J. (2008) *Look Me in the Eyes.* New York, NY: Three Rivers Press.

Rozakis, L. (2002) *Super Study Skills.* New York, NY: Scholastic, Inc.

Shore, S. (2004) *Ask and Tell: Self-Advocacy and Disclosure for People on the Autism Spectrum.* Shawnee Mission, KS: Autism Asperger Publishing Company.

SUBJECT INDEX

AUTHOR INDEX